Self-love is everywhere... so much so that it's easy for the underlying beliefs and emotions it stirs up inside of you to go undetected. In *Starving the Fairytale*, Emily Copeland clearly identifies culture's obsession with self that competes for pieces of your mind and heart and points you to the only love and discovery that will ever fully satisfy you - the knowledge and love of Christ.

Michelle Myers and Somer Phoebus, co-founders and co-authors of *She Works His Way*

What happens when the reasons we do what we do are based on an illusion and fairytale? What happens when what sounds good actually leads us farther from who we were meant to be? In *Starving the Fairytale*, Emily Copeland brings these fairytales before the light one by one, calling out the subtle lies that are holding our lives in check through scripture. Her story shows us how to truly discover and live out this newfound identity in Christ.

Steve Carter, Pastor and Author of *The Thing Beneath The Thing*

In *Starving the Fairytale*, Emily beautifully weaves her personal story of binge eating and hating her body into a practical guide of embracing who God uniquely created her to be. No one does a better job of showing us the dangers of our dead-end journey to self and guiding us back to a path of freedom, truth, and healing that only comes from our relationship with God.

Brandi Wilson, Leading and Loving It

Emily is real, authentic, and writes the truth in love. She's the big sister we all wish we had to guide us through our feelings to the Truth. In *Starving the Fairytale*, she meets us where we are or where we were and takes us on a journey to discover God while breaking down the narrative the world offers us about being enough. This book is for you if you are ready to discover who you really are in Him.

Jessica Hottle Author, Speaker, Coach at jessicahottle. com

D1366510

STARVING
THE
FAIRYTALE

A new model for self-discovery

EMILY COPELAND

To request permissions, contact the publisher at emilyacopeland@gmail.com.

Paperback: 978-0-578-38233-3

First paperback edition May 2022

Edited by Michael Brooks
Cover Art by Evelyn Jagesar
Layout by Allison Capps
Photographs by Evelyn Jagesar

Printed by Amazon KDP
www.amazon.com

To Hadley Love and Willow Grace,

Who you are isn't determined by a journey, but the journey is determined by who you already are in Jesus. May the mirror be a reminder of the grace that stares back. And may you see a girl who is whole, loved, and fully free…all because of Jesus. When your dad and I see you, we see Him. You are already enough.

STARVING THE FAIRYTALE

FOREWORD
BY EVELYN JAGESAR

The woman and her relationship with herself is undoubtedly a centerpiece in our culture. It's everywhere you look, in all corners of culture, from music videos to new diet ads by influencers on Instagram to magazine covers in the grocery aisles. You can't spend five minutes on TV without a commercial selling something via women's sex appeal or without seeing a show covertly or overtly impart something to women about their self-image. There are articles, books, and even studies that point out the obvious problem we've got on our hands here regarding how bombarded women are with these messages left and right like I just did.

You could say it's gotten "better" in recent decades. That there's been a newfound feminism that analyzes the cultural problem we have and that there's been a shift that favors women. Sure. But what isn't talked about is how many pro-women conversations in our culture today still drag women back into believing something untrue about our relationship with our bodies, self-image, and overall sense of self-worth–except it just has a more positive rebranded spin.

Now, women are offered a narrative of saving themselves from the litany of negative messages by finding self-love, self-confidence, self-empowerment. It all sounds pretty good until it doesn't work, and again, women are quietly drowning in ideas of who they are and who they should be. Still weary. Still searching. Now we're supposed to solve the problem we've been given by being our own biggest fan on top of it? The narrative, without the nice fonts and perfect smiles, says it's your fault if you feel powerless to your fill in the blank: weight, career, marriage, family, daily routine, whatever it is, and the only one who can save you is you.

Something in us knows this doesn't feel right, but how did we get here? Why are women trying out idea after idea in search of something that feels true while lacking a compass to navigate True North? Unfortunately, a lot of us are going at this alone. We women don't always grow up with someone ahead of us, intentionally walking our hearts through these deep-running rivers tied to our identity, even though we learn subconsciously how to be a woman from the women around us. And it's not common to find an environment to foster meaningful, healthy conversations that stick through adulthood.

But what about church? Unfortunately, too many Christian contexts don't offer a strong or specific enough voice to combat the story women are hearing everywhere else and show them the rich truth God has instead. When we look left and right, maybe we're surrounded mostly by women who exemplify self-effacement, an overemphasis of serving their bodies into oblivion and making less of themselves, and never really knowing what being made in His image means for them personally.

So, we women often collect a hodgepodge of "self" ideas through experiences, relationships, and influences that are both subtle and screaming, and we have no lens to filter them through. And worse, we collect moments of failure and self-hatred that continue to beat down on us, making us prone to unknowingly accept nice-sounding untruths about ourselves to soothe the internal critic.

Enter Emily Copeland, the big sister who has worn the garments of self-hatred like a heavy cloak and born the burdens that come with it. Enter Emily Copeland, the pastor-hearted mother of two girls who has a perspective to share based on truth. Enter Emily Copeland, the friend to many who champions all walks of life regardless of your beliefs or past. Enter Emily Copeland, a fiercely joyful woman who has been given a weapon to wield against powerful narratives that deceive women into a never-ending battle with herself. Enter Emily Copeland, a conversation sparker and food-for-thought giver who has a message to share with women everywhere, including you who are reading this.

You. What's your story? Maybe you're crushing your workouts and pursuing a passion, but fear slipping up even for one day. Perhaps you compare yourself to others accidentally when you go on social media and haven't connected where that random self-hatred comes from. Maybe you're a Christian who thinks there's no connection between faith and the womanhood culture has said so much about. Perhaps you've denounced faith sources altogether and found yourself in new rhythms of meditation or nature that make you feel connected to your body like no faith source has offered you before. Maybe you haven't paid much thought to what experiences, relationships, and influences are guiding your sense of self, but now you're starting to ask questions.

Can I ask you to put all of the things you've heard before and adopted about yourself in a box? A box in front of you that's separate from your current self reading this, like a bunch of clothes from your closet that you've loved and worn throughout the years? This isn't a Marie Kondo moment where we try them all on and see what sparks joy. This book, *Starving the Fairytale*, is inviting you into a full-blown perspective overhaul. Getting rid of clothes is one thing, but asking what influenced us to buy them in the first place is the kind of heart exercise this book is all about.

It takes bravery to write what Emily has written. Her words are a dare in the face of an invisible beast, an anchor in a rip current. It's clear between the lines of her writing that her intention is to unfold clarity before the reader's eyes, throw a knife through the veil of deceit, and beckon a wake-up call. Within even the first pages of the introduction, you're about to read, that's what happened to me. I can't unsee the thread between all the experiences, relationships, and influences I've accepted as truth about myself: the Fairytale.

If you're ready to be present for this kind of overhaul, continue on. Pause and take moments to reflect as you read and resonate. Let the chills run across your body like they did mine as I devoured word after word of bold truth and purged the weight of self-hatred and self-care models that never satisfied. Write out what you uncover about the Fairytale and reprogram those details to this new model that will sustain you. The process may not be quick or comfortable, but now you will have that anchor, compass, and weapon of truth to wield.

You will need this weapon. As you unravel your ideas of self and try to pick apart the messages you've ingested, the harder it will be to let them go. The hold these untruths have in our hearts and minds is truly like every metaphor Emily will present you. You may not realize how far into the Fairytale you are. You may be offended by the words to come, and maybe not instantly, but as you process her words over time and hear them in your head as you go about your daily life. The truth may hurt as it confronts layer upon layers of the Fairytale, but the truth will set you free.

And if there's one thing I can say this book is about, it's true freedom.

"For whoever wants to save their life will lose it, but whoever loses their life for me will find it."
– Matthew 16:25 NIV

INTRODUCTION

Hating my Body While Trying to Love Jesus

My eyebrows angled, pulling together in a scowl, and I
let out a guttural "ugh!" How could a mirror reflection feel like
a betrayal? Like an enemy invading my personal space, my body
felt like an imposter. How long would this stranger stick around?
She was uncomfortable and heavy. I hated the way she felt and
the way she moved. I spent about four years hating my body.

I held a cold, damp washcloth on my eyes hoping it
would take away the swelling from last night's binge of food
and tears. But nothing could hide my puffy face the way clothes
could cloak my fluffy body. I wiggled into jeans that used to fit
but now felt suffocating. I had never hated a button on a pair of
pants so much. Getting the button in the loophole had become
a miniature game of tug-of-war. I scrambled to find a flowy
top to hide my new and expanding love handles and my arms
that were no longer toned or lean. With one final glance in the
mirror, I winced at the stranger staring back. I walked out of the
door to head to class, already planning my "great escape" back
to the gym to run off all of the evil calories I had eaten the day
before. I needed to sweat away the shame and the agony that
I felt inside. I could control my miles logged even if I couldn't
control my pant size.

Those four years were particularly dark. My body had
changed so much from the thin, eat-whatever-you-want-with-no-
mpact-on-the-scale body. I had gained over 30 pounds in less
han a year. How could I have let this happen? The scale sent
ne spiraling. The number followed me everywhere. How could
a number cause so much damage? I was constantly bloated
and swollen. I suffered awful stomachaches from the moment

I would wake up each day because of the anxiety of it all. The doctors called it IBS. I called it an ambush. I craved food at all hours of the day, but I was ashamed of every single bite of food I put into my mouth. I was sure that others would watch me eat in total disgust. There was not a minute in the day that I didn't think about my body. When I was talking to someone, I'd be thinking about how I wished they didn't have to look at me. It wasn't my body. I didn't recognize it or feel connected to it in any way. It was far from the body that I had once known to be carefree and—honestly, at this point—functional. I tried to starve myself every day (which I'm really bad at, by God's grace). This led to binging, and the cycle would continue over and over again.

Throughout the day, hunger pangs would send shockwaves through my body. I felt victorious over them like I was winning a war. I rejoiced at their presence because it meant that I still had a sliver of control and an ounce of dignity—that I was on my way to feeling worthy of people's glances again. I climbed into bed many afternoons, in between classes, to sleep. Not because I was tired, but because I didn't want to be awake anymore to the temptation of food or to the noise in my head, trying to unscramble the mess of emotions and embarrassment. In the evenings, I would eat dinner like a bear coming out of hibernation. I couldn't stop eating. I couldn't stop craving. I couldn't stop the cycle. When I think of my freshman year of college, I don't think first about the fun time I had living out of state and going to an amazing school. I think about the ache of how much I wanted to look different and how much I wanted to love myself.

While deeply despising my body, I was trying to love Jesus well at the same time.

The Story Will Come Out of Our Greatest Insecurities

It's human to care so much about what others think. My insecurity was how my body looked. Your insecurity may be something different, like not having enough love from a parent, fighting a learning disability or unbearable depression, or facing a season of life in which you feel hopelessly stuck.

This will be no shock to you, but loathing my body and trying to honor Jesus didn't mix well. Have you been here too? I spent a lot of my prayer time begging God to give me more control over my food cravings and that the miles that I was logging on the treadmill would start showing better results. But when you're so stressed over something—especially over your body—your body doesn't cooperate. Was it that I wasn't praying the right thing? Was I not trusting God enough?

Turns out, God and I wanted different things. He wanted my full attention, and I wanted a better body. Was getting my younger, thinner body back too much to ask? No. Was it the most important change that needed to happen in my life at the time? Also, no. I understand the struggle of hating yourself or a part of yourself that you can't seem to change. My body-loathing college season changed the way that I saw myself, the way I saw other people, and ultimately, how I saw God. I didn't believe that other people could love me fully as I was, and it impacted how much energy I gave to Jesus. It kept me drowning in envy for those who didn't seem to have body image issues. I wanted to stay "hidden" until I could pull myself back together. I might as well have pulled my college major out of a hat like a giveaway drawing; I didn't know what I wanted to do, and my mind was working harder to try to figure out how to fix my appearance, not my future profession. I didn't want to hate myself anymore. And, if God wouldn't fix that, then I needed to find my own solution.

This was right before the "love your body" message really began to take mainstream media by storm. I grew up in the low-fat, fat-free, sugar-free, and aerobics era of the '90s. If your body wasn't thin, it meant that there was a problem. This was before plus-size models were on the covers of magazines and before plus-size clothing had its own section at Target.

Most women today would say, with the best intentions, that I deserved to be happy in my own skin and to feel confident no matter what I looked like back then. Women today would quickly come to my defense and encourage me to live how I want to and ignore the haters around me or the negative self-talk inside of my head. Looking back, college Emily would have given every last penny to that message of deep and life-changing "self-love." Oh, how freeing it would be! I wanted so much to be happy in my own skin and to feel free and confident in my body. I wanted to feel seen, and I really wanted to feel like I belonged somewhere. Unbeknownst to me, I wasn't my own worst enemy. This was the plan of my real enemy the entire time. Satan enticed me with a focus so sharply toward myself that I felt like a foreigner in my own world. My own insecurities kept me isolated. My own insecurities kept me staring into the mirror. I didn't like what I saw, but I couldn't look away. I couldn't escape it. The person looking back at me was the only person that I cared about at the time. I wanted her to change more than anything in the world. As the self-hatred grew, my focus sharpened. Determination to change me became my drug.

Who was I then? What was at the root of my addiction to binging and then starving? Why couldn't I control it? And where could I find the self-love that I needed to overcome this monster? I didn't know where to go, but I knew I had to figure it out. Little did I know that a story full of illusion was taking shape on the pages of my life.

The Fairytale of Self as God

It seems like I had fallen into some kind of pre-set script for my life. For the sake of not burning out on the terms, "self-love" or "self-discovery," I will call this script the fairytale. The fairytale is a heroic story given to every girl and woman, full of promised love and adventure, with only one hero. And in my case, that hero was a heroine: me. From the depths of my self-loathing, my intense and hyper-focus on myself would eventually turn into an obsession with myself. (If you're like me, you probably just sang the line, "Why you so obsessed with me?" by Mariah Carey in your head.) The more work that I set out to do, the more I would open up to the world of self-empowerment that would lead to the self-love I wanted. I would become who I thought I needed to be all on my own.

The fairytale was taking form. I believed that I could single-handedly learn to love myself enough, by means of a better body, to fill all the broken gaps in my life. I believed that other people would approve of me as I hit milestones. I believed that God was holding out on me here in my unfamiliar body. Deep down, I felt shackled to my insecurities, creating the perfect setup for the fairytale to weave its web into my heart. The fairytale would make me the hero, saving me from myself and from the cruel world around me. But was the fairytale of self-discovery my only option to feel free in my own skin?

The fairytale always begins with the first few steps down the self-discovery path, figuring out who we are and what we need and desire most. The lie takes root from there, convincing us that we deserve to "find ourselves" at any cost to meet our needs and desires. The fairytale ends with us, me and you, as the heroines, the untouchable and most lovable characters. It's a promise of a happy-ever-after ending because it tells us that we can reach our full potential without any help from anyone else. In the end, you and I find ourselves on the throne. In the end, we are the gods of our own life.

The best part of every fairytale is the moment that the lead character finds love and gets to keep it, right? Don't we all deserve love? This pre-set script of the fairytale in my own life claimed it would put me on a direct path of love. It promised that if I could choose to love myself without any conditions, and if I could commit to a continued self-discovery work effort, that I would find the pot of happiness at the end of the rainbow. The fairytale didn't even ask me to submit to anyone else. I didn't have to ask for permission or to yield to a "higher power." That higher power would simply be me.

Spoiler alert: I never got to my dream bodyweight. I didn't fall in love with myself because of the work I put in. I haven't gained so much self-confidence that I don't still feel self-conscious or awkward in a bathing suit. The fairytale message says that we can achieve a love for ourselves that is void of insecurity, doubt, wanting more, or working to maintain what we have become. It offers a perceived perfect ending to a disappointing beginning.

The fairytale also delivers a lie that there are people who have achieved self-love allowing them to discover deeper levels of themselves, to uncover their deepest needs, and that gives them the confidence that they can satisfy all of those needs themselves. It is attractive because it touches us in our pain and promises a new story with a much better ending. The lie of the fairytale wafts the hope of peace that passes understanding through the air like fragrance coming out of a perfume bottle. The truth is that there is not one person on the planet who is 100% happy with who she is every moment of every day. (Did I even have to say it?) The fairytale journey that so many women are launching themselves on without Jesus is one that is full of continued illusion. To be blunt, the fairytale itself is an illusion. And, for the record, the illusion doesn't look good on us.

In total opposition to the illusion that the world projects onto us, A.W. Tozer[1] in his book The Pursuit of God says, "Every soul belongs to God and exists by His pleasure." We can't ignore God and our very reason for existence and find total peace on our own accord. God has a better way for us, and we're about to unwrap it like a gift on Christmas morning.

Here's where we are headed. The goal of our time together is to illuminate the illusion and its cheap messaging that is drawing us women into a dead-end journey of self. We will hold that illusion against the Light of Truth and, together, fully follow Jesus. It's time to Starve the Fairytale before it finishes starving us. Let's go.

---

[1] Tozer, A.W. 2015. Pursuit of God. Abbotsford, Wi: Aneko Press.

1 THE DANGER

If you have social media, you've been exposed to the fairytale. This isn't a problem reserved only for the weak or the young. We cannot blame our current selfish culture on Gen Z while we spend most of our time looking into a screen full of illusion too. Every five minutes on social media, someone is declaring themselves a whole new person. I've seen women of all ages trying every product, herb, drug, meditation, crystal, therapy, etc. on the planet, and for most of them, they have a "success" story. A story in which seeking a deeper connection with themselves has brought them freedom in some way. I do not doubt that they have had a transformation that has impacted their life, but the illusion is that it has solved all of their problems, clearing the way to endearing self-love and confidence that is unmatched and never wavers. Those of us onlookers find ourselves wondering if we could have this too.

Dare I say that the illusion of total peace and happiness within ourselves begins with someone else's perceived success? If it's working for her, it must be worth trying. If she is that happy, I must try it, too. Social media has spread "hope" through mediums of all kinds like a disease. We wonder why people are getting further and further away from God right now. It's the illusion of achieving better within ourselves. It's the perception of beautiful green grass on the other side. And what's the cost? Hardly anything from the looks of it—just spend more time with yourself. Invest further into the things that make you happy. Sounds like a dream! Most illusions do. Quick assessment: If you can control the end game, then what you're dealing with is a fairytale. Let me explain; I believed that committing to a workout program would bring me results that would, in turn, bring me peace and happiness about my appearance. I had small victories that gave me hope in the process. My goals felt achievable for that moment, but as soon as I messed up, the line of my goal moved further ahead. It's like homeownership; you fix one thing and then something else breaks. Real happiness and peace apart from God are fluid goals, no matter what your friends on social media say.

Self-love and a solid self-care system seem like the most logical, practical, and essential options. College Emily would have given anything to have the discipline of self-care that would give way to the self-love that I'd craved. Most people would cry foul on anyone saying that self-love is not the most logical answer to any problem. In our weakest moments, we search for the thing that can help us most. For many of us, when we find things that work temporarily, we become tempted to give more of ourselves to the power they seem to hold.

Why are Women Chasing the Fairytale, and Why Is It So Dangerous?

Between you and me, I wanted to write a book of encouragement and just talk about the goodness of Jesus for 50,000 words. But, through experiences with friends, watching women on social media, and simply being tuned into culture, God laid this conversation on my heart, and I haven't been able to shake it. I have watched Jesus-followers turn inward to pursue inner peace and satisfaction when He didn't come through for them. I have watched young girls begin reciting messages like, "I'm working on being more selfish with my time to find peace within my day." I've seen influencers gathering large crowds of women into their meditation practices and rituals, honoring themselves and nature, but never God. I see many, many confused Christians who have direct access to their Creator and Designer wondering how they can love themselves more. Record numbers of women are changing their worldviews and their beliefs about God in exchange for the wide road of acceptance and neutrality. This isn't just a personal problem. This is a pandemic for souls.

The hyper-focus on self has ironically become a treasured journey that many Christian women are fully embracing at an alarming rate. Understanding ourselves and harnessing the power and control of our lives is the new goal that nothing and no one should come between. The tricky thing about power is that the most powerful person is the one at the very, very top. As created beings, we are not actually the ones at the very, very top. There is a power hierarchy that is flipped; creation (us) is trying to elevate, heal, and restore itself. Creation is playing god without God. Imitation of the power of God isn't flattery; it's fatal.

How can a journey of self-discovery be fatal? How can pursuing the deepest levels of self-love be an illusion? When the story ends with us, and not with God, then our discoveries were merely imitations of the real thing. How sad it would be to get to the end of your life to realize you spent the entire time looking in the mirror. But the journey of finding one's "truest" or "happiest" self is a lonely, solo trip that leads only to the end of this life with nothing to show for.

The self-journey movement is already etched into the pages of Scripture. Romans 1:25 says, "*They exchanged the truth of God for a lie, and worshiped and served the creature rather than the Creator.*" This is idolatry's well-crafted lie: us thinking we can put ourselves in the place of God or at least be equal to Him in power and control over our own lives. This is the "lie" from Satan that cast all of humanity under sin's curse. That lie is found in Genesis 3:1-5:

> *Now the serpent was more crafty than any of the wild animals the Lord God had made. He said to the woman, "Did God really say, 'You must not eat from any tree in the garden'?" The woman said to the serpent, "We may eat fruit from the trees in the garden, but God did say, 'You must not eat fruit from the tree that is in the middle of the garden, and you must not touch it, or you will die.'" "You will not certainly die," the serpent said to the woman. "For God knows that when you eat from it your eyes will be opened, and you will be like God, knowing good and evil."*

The lie was simple: you can and will be like God.

To be clear, most women today aren't looking in the mirror and saying, "Yes, today I think I've outdone God." In fact, our culture would ignore the very thought of God. But, to be our "highest selves," we have to position our desires above anything or anyone else. This inward work doesn't "out-work" God; it replaces Him altogether.

When the Apostle Paul wrote Romans 1:25, he didn't write this to a culture that agreed with Him. The Roman empire was sexually vile and living for (literally) anything that felt good to them. This passage is speaking about any sin that honors the pleasure or love of self. When self-love is more important than God's love, or when we are obsessed with the things we want to change about ourselves, without realizing it, we worship the creature (us) rather than the Creator. We find ourselves in a funhouse of mirrors, chasing the best version of ourselves. But God has never asked us to find the best version of ourselves. Instead, He gifted us with that opportunity when He gave up His own life through Jesus for us and invited us to take up a cross and die to self with him. The best version of ourselves is only found in Jesus. It's radical and glorious and graciously real.

So Here We Are...

For a natural-born peacekeeper, exploiting the shiny object of self-discovery that everyone loves and helping women take the blinders off to a journey leading to no-(wo)man's land is extra uncomfortable for me. But it's past due.

This book was written out of concern for all women, especially Christian women. I finally started putting these words to paper the moment that I thought my heart couldn't take it anymore. Another one down. Another woman I love embracing the idea that she is more intuitive and able to understand herself more than her Creator understands her—more than the One who physically put her pieces together, who counted the hairs He would put on her head. The One who made her short or tall, muscular or lean, black or brown, strong-willed or quiet. The One who chose her parents, her environment, and her moment in history. The One who gave her that first breath and who has controlled every breath since. The One who would see her tears when no one else could, who would work out her circumstances and watch her give the credit to luck instead. The One who has been waiting for her to come back home and to recognize her first Love as her greatest gift. God Himself.

But He's got competition. In fact, He's losing. Not because He doesn't have the power, but because we believe the "Garden of Eden" lie that we can prosper without Him.

God's not losing Christian women to an inherently bad idea, at least not on the surface. No, this is where the darkness has some sparkle to it, because it looks like the best version of us. The enemy knows that he doesn't have to look far today, he just has to make sure that women keep looking in the mirror, not Scripture.

Our enemy is wicked smart. He knows that he can get us to where he wants us if we are given small, incremental choices that are just a degree or two off of the path. It doesn't start with denying God. Our wandering can start with a simple self-care message that feels like a necessity in our lives and one to which we give space regularly. Self-care isn't a bad thing. (Trust me; we will flesh this out together in the upcoming chapters.) But let me show you the progression that can quickly follow when left unchecked: **Self-care turns into self-discovery, self-love, self-acceptance, self-reliance, and then self as god.** Self-care without fully relying on God for sustenance and fulfillment sets the journey off by a single degree. Self-care can be a responsibility, but it is not our redeemer. Self-care should fall in the category of brushing your teeth and getting to the gym. Self-care, with the intention of healing our weary and broken parts, paired with the mindset of "I can do it all by myself," is a spark that can light a room but can also quickly grow into a wildfire that burns down the whole house. Self-care may help with temporary relief, but only God can provide total healing and restoration. More on this to come. Will you explore this topic with me?

Most of us didn't purposely choose to step into a self-journey, at least not initially. Those lies chose us because our enemy is out to steal, kill, and destroy (John 10:10). The journey, for many of us, begins with the intrigue of the subtle messaging that exists all around us. The messaging of self-first is woven so tightly into our culture that we really don't know anything else. We will unpack this messaging in much greater detail in the chapters to come, put it under the lens of scripture, and refuse to let it penetrate our heart if it doesn't meet God's standard of love. Our goal is to be able to spot this messaging a mile away. This is a real battle over our soul and our purpose. We can't afford to let the enemy gain any more ground.

When the world says to choose the journey of the self, Jesus calls us to choose spiritual poverty.

Spiritual Poverty and Sermon on the Mount

Right after Jesus called His apostles and right before He sent them out to do the work, He told them how they could be blessed. The very first thing He told them was, *"blessed are you who are poor, for yours is the kingdom of God"* (Luke 6:20).

Jesus knew that humanity would try to stand on its own two feet and walk to the rhythm of its own power and spiritual resources. But He wasn't talking about money, rather being poor spiritually— understanding that God holds the power, not us. We may have nothing to show spiritually, but we can hold everything we need at the very same time because of Jesus.

Thinking that we have our own spiritual, mental, or emotional resources through social media influencers, "spiritual gurus", podcasts, mentorship classes, or retreats that are capable of more healing power than the power of God is an illusion, and it's getting many women nowhere really, really fast.

It's in social media in which women have displayed

illusions of the ideal life, unwavering confidence, put-together families, and the strength (and time) to do it all. So, the rest of us have watched on the sidelines, trying to implement their ways and follow in their footsteps. We've tried the trends, taken their advice, and struggled to pull ourselves out of crippling discouragement when none of it has worked for us. Social media created a new level of the self-obsessed roller coaster, and here we are still trying to enjoy the ride that is making us sick.

How many of us would admit that putting our life on display, whether in front of 100 followers or 1 million, has left us feeling empty-handed? In the process of trying to "find ourselves" and make something of ourselves on social media, have we found the kind of healing, restoration, and freedom that we were hoping we would find? For so many of us who would answer "no," we may have moved on to a "personal" and "internal" journey. How can we compete with other women? A.W Tozer again, wisely says, "As long as you set yourself up as a little god to which you must be loyal there will be those who will delight to offer offense to your idol. How then can you hope to have inward peace?"[2] Even as you invest energy to better yourself, there will always be others doing better than you. So we pursue an "internal" journey that is even more devastating than a public journey because it's here, in the isolation of our mind and thoughts, where we lose accountability and where we lose the ability for others to speak truth into our lives. It's here that we are encouraged to go find our own truth, and in that, we can come up with some crazy stuff. When our past hurts meet our present reality, we are not prepared to tackle it on our own. We've all experienced some really wild things in life—some more traumatic than others—and as the creation of our Creator, human beings standing before a Designer God, we don't actually hold the tools to fix ourselves. If we did, then Jesus wasted His time and His life. If we can fix ourselves, then what's the point of heaven? If we could fix ourselves, our world wouldn't be so fractured and frail.

Tozer, A.W. 2015. Pursuit of God. Abbotsford, Wi: Aneko Press.

It's time to starve the self-first culture, and I hope that you'll go there with me. It's going to require (ironically) a self-evaluation to ensure that you've not been enchanted by the fairytale. You may find yourself completely offended by the words of this intro or the words to come. In fact, you may even think that I'm narrow-minded or intolerant. But I can assure you that there is love and angst on these pages to see you live the life you were designed to live. Can I implore you to press on? Can you commit to finishing the book to see the glory of hope that will be revealed to you? Quite frankly, being offended can keep us stuck in lies. Be willing to continue when it stings. Galatians 5:1 says, *"It is for freedom that Christ has set us free. Stand firm, then, and do not let yourselves be burdened again by a yoke of slavery."* In sharing my own brokenness of hating the very skin I lived in, I hope to take your hand and show you what God has taught me; there is unbelievable hope for our future with Christ because He can redeem anyone and anything. There is rest and rejuvenation that will blow your mind when you are in relationship with your Creator. Take heart, you will not read the last page of this book without understanding Who really has your back. Hint: it's not the people behind the clever, positive affirmation marketing campaigns of your favorite beauty or fitness products.

Through honest evaluation of the content of this book, we are all in for a radical awakening and a transformation that will impact generations that come after us. Are we willing to ask ourselves honestly where we currently stand? Are we willing to do the work? We are going to tackle big things together in this book. But, when we link arms and when our Creator and Father God is the Prize we are after, mountains can move, and people will finally and fully be free. You can finally and fully be free.

2 THE GIRLS

At fifteen years old, and with a tall, awkward, and lanky body, I signed onto a modeling agency in Chicago. My mom had a friend who was a very successful model in the '80s who encouraged me to connect with Elite Model Management, the second most sought-after agency in the world at the time. I was fourteen when we first sent pictures to the agency. We heard back from them immediately, and for almost a year we sent pictures to them every month because they had to wait until I was fifteen in order to sign with me. I'll never forget the day we drove to Chicago to officially sign my contract. We drove straight to McDonald's after the signing where I proceeded to pound a Big Mac meal and a large Coke without a single thought or care about it.

Within two weeks of signing, I got my first job. I went on location in New York with Abercrombie Kids and ended up in the wall-size photo in every store around the world. In the early 2000s where I grew up, Abercrombie was a really big deal. Even my dentist asked for the Abercrombie poster to put up in his waiting room. (Just to make that statement a little less weird, I was smiling in the photo, and it was a great shot of my teeth, which he was proud of).

Shortly afterward, I won a very competitive and exclusive modeling contest out of Miami in which celebrities and NBA stars attended. I flew to Singapore and competed for a $250,000 contract against fifty girls from all over the world. I continued to work for big-name stores and brands and worked with celebrities over the next few years. I even moved to Chicago for a summer between my Junior and Senior year of high school to work. I then graduated high school a semester early with plans to work out of Miami at my agency there.

But once I turned eighteen, at the peak of my modeling career, my body changed. I didn't stay thin and lanky. As hard as I tried (which included many unhealthy tactics to stay thin and avoid eating), I couldn't stay thin. My agents asked if I wanted to gain a few more pounds and become a part of the plus-size division. In 2006, plus-size was still a smaller size than you could ever imagine. The "plus-size" requirement was distorted because it represented anyone who wasn't ultra-skinny, model-size.

I didn't go to Miami because of internal changes that happened at the agency, but really, God was at work. So I spent the last semester of my senior year of high school at home, trying to avoid my hunger and get my body back to skin and bones.   But, it was too late. I had begun to spiral, and the darkness of despising myself was closing in. I had a million things that I told myself each day: "You're disgusting and out of control"; "You've completely failed"; "No one will love you like this"; "You're such a joke." I resigned from the agencies at the end of my senior year of high school and went to college.

Instead of reaching my agency's goal of the New York runway and my personal goal of a long-term and successful modeling career, I spent the next two years in school and the following two years as a newly married 20-year-old woman, hating myself and what I had become. I begged God to help me like myself. I asked Him to either give me the self-control to stop binge-eating to lose weight or to find a way to love my body as it was, but I never fully surrendered my ways to His will. I was trying to love and serve Him, but the way I viewed my body held me captive to myself.

My top priority was to find a way to love myself because I couldn't stand myself. Self-care methods of getting to the gym, eating as healthy (and as little) as I could, embracing the kind and encouraging words of my friends and family, and, of course, treating myself to an indulgent treat whenever I felt sad seemed like a good idea. But they never fully delivered. The Band-Aid of self-care kept me stuck. It kept my feet planted in front of the mirror, forcing me to stare at myself, the girl who had one soul desire: to love myself by any means necessary. The more desperate I became to find self-love, the more I found myself in front of the mirror trying to fix and change myself. God didn't have very much room in my heart because, frankly, there was just too much of me there to fit anyone else.

I was swept into the current of the fairytale message. The same message that has consumed our culture consumed me: that the best version of you and I are all that we need in this life. The most important person to know is yourself. The most important work you can do is to work on yourself. The fairytale of the self-first life is captivating and mesmerizing like every good fairytale is. We don't have to start far away from God to end up in this place. In fact, we may fully believe that God is Healer and still feel the pull of the fairytale story over our lives, that we can be fully enough without God and simply add Him in as needed along the way.

Your story may not include a season of unwanted weight gain and wrestling of identity like mine. I fed the fairytale for a long time out of desperation to feel accepted and approved by the world. You may have found yourself desperately wanting to love the person that God made you to be some other way. The offer of the fairytale isn't only reserved for those who are experiencing their darkest hours. The fairytale doesn't discriminate at all, and that's why being able to identify it is so vital to a healthy life and relationship with God and yourself. Listen, Adam and Eve were living in a literal perfect world in the Garden of Eden when they bought into the fairytale. Their bodies, environment, food sources, and relationships with God were perfect when they were approached by Satan. So, even on our very best day, the fairytale exists and is begging to write your story onto its pages.

To help you see how the fairytale is unfolding in different ways for women today, I wanted to tell you the stories of three women I know. With their names changed for obvious reasons, these women, I believe, represent all of us in unique ways. These women have come face to face with the fairytale, just like you and me. Lean in, and let their stories connect you to the way that the self-first journey is influencing all of us in our current culture.

Meet the Girls

Alissa is a vibrant and beautiful twenty-eight year old. She grew up in an environment that had very few rules. Alissa was always well-loved by her family and friends, but her parents were disconnected, busy, and lacked a spiritual belief system of any kind. Church was something that her parents felt unworthy of attending most of the time, so she only went a few times growing up. God was someone that she knew was probably out there, but not someone she assumed she had any chance of really knowing. Alissa, though, was a go-getter. Alissa loved to dream. She knew that if she could just work hard enough, that she would earn money to purchase the things she really wanted.

She worked multiple jobs in high school and paid her own way through community college. All the while, she stuffed emotional and physical trauma deep down inside of her that she had experienced as a young child. It impacted her friendships and relationships as well as her physical health. She worked really hard to stay happy on the outside, but she fought the darkness of feeling worthless on the inside.

In elementary school, Alissa had watched her dad climb into his car, roll down the window, and wave goodbye just like any other day, except that time, he didn't come home. She found out about her parent's divorce about two weeks later. How could a parent walk away from his kids? If her dad couldn't stay, how could anyone else love her? She battled the voices in her head as a teenager, the ones that said she wouldn't be missed if she was gone and that she could end the pain at any time.

She wouldn't consider herself worthy of love and because of that, she didn't love others well. In and out of friendships and dating relationships, she felt as though no one would ever fill that gap in her life. Were real love and connection with anyone else even possible? On top of that, the pressures of society and culture to keep up, to work really hard, and to somehow believe in yourself in the process just wasn't working for her.

One day, a friend who seemed really happy and healthy told her that it wasn't just about believing in herself, but that she had to love herself more than anyone or anything, and this would be the key to finding peace and purpose. Alissa felt those words sink into the deepest part of her. Was this the answer? Was it self-love that she had been missing all along? She had been so discontent her entire life—discontent with her life, her circumstances, and disconnected to a lack of love for herself. It always felt like something was missing. Could genuine self-love be the answer?

It made the most sense. If you hate yourself, that impacts every part of your life. But if you love yourself and invest energy into becoming the best version of yourself, that cannot be the wrong thing, right? So she began to reflect. "Peace comes from within," she was told. She first started to identify what areas she was lacking peace in, and she realized that she wasn't taking great care of herself. First step: self-care.

She knew she needed to fuel her body well with good food and exercise. She followed some Instagram accounts that seemed to offer the cleanest and most nutritious food tips and recipes. Then she took up yoga and Pilates to strengthen her body while also giving her a chance to reflect and meditate. She noticed a huge difference right away! The brain fog of processed foods, refined sugars, and a stagnant lifestyle was lifting, and she felt good for the first time in a long time. She said to herself, "I can totally heal my body and live well. I've made huge strides all by myself—something to be proud of!"

Things were looking up, and she began studying more about the idea of a "self-discovery," a continued journey of understanding what's wrong with oneself in order to self-heal the parts that are broken. If she could make big strides with her health, she knew that tackling the deeper issues would only bring more freedom. She began to love herself for what she could do. Her friends cheered her on as she found ways to accept herself and celebrate the new person that she was.

There really were no rules to self-discovery—if it felt good and made you feel freer, then it was acceptable. Who could stop her or judge her? It was her life, and these were the things that made her happy. Discovering more about herself and working to heal those parts of her instilled a belief that she didn't need anyone else to help her through life; she was fully and completely capable of changing her life and her destiny on her own. She declared herself self-reliant and proud of the independent woman that she was becoming. She didn't need to rely on anyone else to help her grow or heal—she was now in full control of that. Alissa loved to share that the power she had found was always right inside of her.

No person, deity, circumstance, or religious system could honor her the way that she had finally learned to honor herself. She did the work and found a version of peace and happiness in spite of those things.

Candace

Candace is eighteen years old. She has always been a quiet girl who loves to take in the world around her. She's a processor, always analyzing information and impressing her friends with great grades as she chases her dream to become a nurse. She would call herself a perfectionist, reluctantly of course.

Candace has a history of attending church throughout her life and even got involved in the youth group for a short time through some friends who attended. From her time in church, she learned that God loves her and that He is important. She has tried to connect with Him like her youth pastor encouraged her to do. She reads her Bible occasionally but has had a hard time understanding a lot of it. What she did understand from her reading seems very powerful and life-changing. But life is hard, and, as a deep analytical thinker, processor, perfectionist, and naturally anxious person, she faces a constant battle within herself to feel loved and to be acceptable to the world around her. She carries past baggage of impossibly high standards and expectations set by her parents. She carries the wounds of not living up to those expectations, and she has not yet dealt with those wounds.

In order to feel alive and loved, Candace finds escape in the sexual encounters she has with boys her age who show any interest. Her painful reality slips into the background as she transforms into a free spirit around a new guy. The thrill of the chase is her escape. But with every relationship comes a hangover of shame and regret. Hiding her experiences from her parents feels like she is evening out the scoreboard. The double life and hunger to please all of the people around her comes at a price; she has panic attacks often, and waves of depression rock her to her core.

She has been told that faith in God will solve all of those problems. Where has He been in-between her church attendance and the dark moments of shame? Does she need to do her own heart-work to find acceptance within herself? God is love, and Candace believes that God would want her to find that happiness, right? Through social media and influencers that she found on Instagram, she keeps seeing the message that she must first love herself in order to find peace and happiness. In addition, if she loves herself fully, then she can love and serve other people well too. She remembers that the Bible says to "Love your neighbor as yourself." That message computes and makes sense to her. The message that she is seeing all around her is one that is equally as positive; "Be unapologetically YOU!"; "Your power is within you"; "You create your peace"; "Love yourself most." How could a positive message be wrong?

Her analytical mind loves the simplicity of that message and believes that loving herself may just be the way to solve her anxiety and bring her acceptance with herself and others. This is what will set her free and give her confidence to love herself and love her life no matter what happens. The confusion is lifted. If Jesus loves us and tells us to love our neighbor as ourselves, then we need to operate from the position that self-love is a prerequisite to our purpose. Candace listens daily to positive and uplifting podcasts that teach her how to love herself more deeply. She is like a sponge, working hard every day to soak up all of the ways that she can find inner peace, like spending her time outdoors, meditating, reading her Bible occasionally, and speaking daily affirmations over herself. She reposts self-affirming social media posts and is determined to use her career in nursing to help pass the self-love message along to her patients and coworkers.

Asia

Asia is 38 years old. She is a wife and mom to three children. Asia grew up in a Christian family, and her parents were faithful followers of Jesus her entire life. She is a follower of Jesus too who loves Him and runs to Him every day. Asia learned the truth from Scripture at an early age. She is not afraid to speak up, to teach, and to talk about Jesus whenever she has the chance. She's the one who shares the occasional photo of her children on social media but really uses the space to talk about what she is learning in Scripture.

She absolutely loves being a part of her local church. She serves faithfully and leads a Bible study on campus or via Zoom when she has the opportunity. Overall, she is well respected in her spiritual community because of her passion and commitment. She believes that because Jesus loves us, and that it is also very important that we love ourselves. She believes in empowering women through positive self-talk and by teaching about the confidence that comes from knowing Jesus.

In Asia's experience with women in the church and what she is seeing on social media, she is encountering more and more women who are not just discontent with themselves but are beginning to recite the pro-self messages all around them. She hears that they feel like they should love themselves and that the culture of body positivity, dealing with past trauma, and political climate tells them to do so. She is talking with women who are confused about how to live happily, confidently, and with unconditional self-love in order to feel most fulfilled in life. She has told them about Jesus, and they agree that He is important, but they aren't sure that He can fully heal them the way they think they need to be healed.

Asia has grown discouraged and frustrated with the messaging all around her, that women have to first be happy with themselves—no matter what—in order to feel loved by God or anyone else. Women are even saying point-blank that God cannot heal them the way that they have been able to heal themselves. Asia is feeling defeated in her conversations and in what she is seeing in her news feed. To where is the growing trend of self-care leading?

Asia has even spent time considering if loving ourselves is something that God needs us to do. She has been studying Scripture and having conversations with trusted friends and fellow Christians. She feels conflicted about how to approach these conversations. How can she love people well, honor their life experiences, talk about self-love from a biblical perspective, and combat any darkness that may exist all at the same time? Like Asia, before we can figure out how to speak light into the darkness, we must understand how women are discovering the journey of self.

Intentional Self-Journey vs. Unintentional Self-Journey

Have you ever followed your GPS without realizing that it wasn't taking you to the correct destination? You followed your trusty device right into the unknown, only to realize it too late. (I personally blame Apple maps mostly, because Google maps are where it's at, but I digress...)

I have a friend who was driving from the west side of the state of Michigan when she was a teenager, trying to come home to Detroit. She punched in an address into the GPS and just started driving—listening to the directions—trusting the process because that's what you do with a GPS. Without understanding what highways lead to where, she unknowingly hopped on the wrong highway because her GPS told her to. A 3-hour road trip turned into a 5-hour road trip when she ended up in a city about an hour off course.

I can say with confidence that few things would leave me more frustrated and tired than if I missed the mark and found myself miles and miles from home. My friend didn't start off knowing that her path was off course. She trusted the direction of the GPS that seemingly knew more than her. My best guess is that it spoke in an English accent, making it appear even more appealing and knowledgeable. She looked at the GPS directions and thought they looked good, reasonable, and with the fastest route to take her to her desired location—home. She got home safe and sound, shaken by the route that had looked so promising at the start. It was a route, she later realized, that would never have led her home, but only to wander further. She had to work hard, stay alert, and keep hoping and wishing that the wandering would soon end. The voice of the GPS led her, its confidence unwavering with every command, and its voice sounded like one worth following.

When a good-sounding message leads to the wrong place, it's no longer a helpful message; it's just wrong. For the record, we do laugh about this story still today, and she has greatly improved her GPS skills. After all, it takes one good trip gone poorly to evaluate every detail for all of the trips to follow.

At the end of the day, we don't end up in the wrong place because we choose to end up in the wrong place. Even wanderlust moments are planned to some degree, right? We can end up in the wrong place by following what we believe to be right and good as we hope it will bring us the best outcome—whether it's a job we believe to be best only to find out it's an unhealthy working environment. Maybe it's a drink to celebrate a special occasion that leads to more and more until it's an unhealthy habit. We don't typically make bad decisions knowing that they will lead to something destructive, harmful, or unhealthy.

While Alissa and Candace have the best intentions of pursuing what seemingly brings life, hope, freedom, through a deeper connection to self, Asia wonders how to approach women like them and their experiences with the truth of Scripture. She works hard to understand how God would expect her to respond to their personal encounters with the fairytale of self-care and self-love.

All three women have been journeying toward understanding what discovering self in today's age really means for them or for others. Not every self-discovery journey is intentional, though. Like all of us, unintentionally or intentionally, they are searching for the best outcome for their heart and life. In this current time and culture, these three women represent all of us in some way—each coming face to face with the reality that the messaging of culture is forcing a choice: for us to choose self above everything else, which pulls us further from God, or for us to choose God above everything else, which pulls us further away from self. So where does it go wrong? And is it wrong to pursue the discovery of self or to support others in their discovery of self even if you aren't sure what to think about that yet?

To answer those questions, we just need to take it all the way back to our origin, that's all. Whether intentionally or unintentionally, the pursuit of the "highest self" connects us back to the first two human beings ever created. Adam and Eve were told not to eat from one tree in the garden (of thousands, we might imagine), so how could one tree out of so many be so tempting that it would cause Adam and Eve to eat from it anyway? Hint: it wasn't the tree that was enticing; it was the promise of who they could become if they ate from it. The serpent (Satan) told them that God was holding out on them, that He didn't want them to eat from it because if they did, their minds would be opened and they would become their "highest" selves—knowing as much as God, the Creator Himself.

I believe that the fairytale of self-discovery started with one simple statement:

> "The Lord God took the man and put him in the Garden of Eden to work it and take care of it. And the Lord God commanded the man, "You are free to eat from any tree in the garden; but you must not eat from the tree of the knowledge of good and evil, for when you eat from it you will certainly die." Genesis 2:15-17.

How the serpent created a fairytale for Adam and Eve is most important for us to know:

> *Now the serpent was more crafty than any of the wild animals the Lord God had made. He said to the woman, "Did God really say, 'You must not eat from any tree in the garden'?" The woman said to the serpent, "We may eat fruit from the trees in the garden, but God did say, 'You must not eat fruit from the tree that is in the middle of the garden, and you must not touch it, or you will die.'" "You will not certainly die," the serpent said to the woman. "For God knows that when you eat from it your eyes will be opened, and you will be like God, knowing good and evil." When the woman saw that the fruit of the tree was good for food and pleasing to the eye, and also desirable for gaining wisdom, she took some and ate it. She also gave some to her husband, who was with her, and he ate it. Then the eyes of both of them were opened, and they realized they were naked; so they sewed fig leaves together and made coverings for themselves.*
> Genesis 3:1-7

The enemy promised that they would know all things and hold power that they were not originally created to hold within themselves. That's all it took. The promise of a "higher" self, a "true," "happy," "powerful," and "independent" self. Sound familiar? Have you heard this promise or messaging in your social feed or in conversation with friends? Pick up any self-help book and you will find an eerily similar message. Spoiler alert: achieving their "highest selves" didn't happen. Adam and Eve's determined self-discovery removed them from God's presence and set the entire human race into the broken state in which it will remain until Christ's return.

I'm no different than any other woman. I've believed that I could be happier with myself if I could just know myself enough to change for the better. I've believed that I could love myself more if I just loved myself as I am. These beliefs take a lot of confidence, but they don't require very much truth. In their perfection, God never invited Adam and Eve to discover the best versions of themselves because He simply assigned it to them through His image.

We are working a lot harder than we have to find the "best" version of ourselves. How do I know? Because I spent years on the hunt and still find myself often trying to look for it again.

The Story Isn't Over

No story is without hope until it's over. We may just be looking for hope in the wrong place right now. I once heard a pastor in Dallas, TX who said, "God has been working and fixing our mess ever since the Garden of Eden." The entire Bible is a story of God fixing the mess that Adam and Eve made. He sent His Perfect Son from heaven into our mess to fix the unfixable. 1 John 4:9 says, *"This is how God showed his love among us: He sent his one and only Son into the world that we might live through him."*

So, if God is out to fix a self-obsessed culture, we should be too. And we can start with ourselves. Alissa, Candace, and Asia—you and I too—are not yet lost beyond hope, even if the path is taking us in a direction that won't lead us to the safety of home or truth. As a very body-conscious college aged-girl, on a journey of self-destruction, my story wasn't over. Today, as I walk on a path that God has created for me and write a book about the self-care journey in order to hold it up under the light of Scripture, my story is not over. Searching for contentment, living in confusion, and fighting conflict are going to be a part of my story, just like it will continue to be a part of yours. Even in a culture that is saturated in the messaging of a life lived for self, there is hope.

But we have to walk through the hard things; we are going to uncover so much together. Why? Because the stories of Alissa, Candace, and Asia represent all of us. They are our friends, our family, our coworkers. Many Christ-followers like Asia are concerned, discouraged, and fearful of how many girls and women will slowly fade into the self-discovery rip current and never escape. We are tackling the fairytale head-on because women are leaving the church. They are walking away from faith. They are slowly letting their walls down to the enemy without realizing it. We are tackling the fairytale because of the women outside of the church who haven't had a chance to hear the greatest story that has ever been told. They are trying to do the best that they can do with what they have, and what they have is a message of light and life and love—but one that is not coming from the truth of God's word. These girls and ourselves are trying to navigate something beautiful, yet destructive; empowering, yet crippling; hope-filled, yet ripping us away from the Source of all Life.

The basic desire that I had to love myself has been exposed by culture. We are all being exposed and now being forced to choose the path that we will take. Will we choose to put ourselves first or will God get that spot in our lives? You must know that there is great hope in that question and in the chapters ahead. Why? Because even though fairytales aren't real, there is a God who is real and who wants to protect your life from fanciful stories. God is a God of truth and reality.

As we starve the fairytale of a lifetime spent admiring ourselves in the mirror, we will begin to see the other story that exists.

We crave the romance of the fairytale life, the infatuation with someone who is better than our wildest dreams. We want to be rescued, whisked off of our feet, and loved without condition. But we won't find someone who is better than our wildest dreams in the fairytale of self-love. We find it in someone who put us all together and planned out our life before the air ever hit our lungs.

What's even better? God designed us for romance. God put romance in our hearts from the get-go. It's a romance that can only be quenched by its most intimate source of life and love and hope. The fairytale version of life is an overly romanticized version of us in love with ourselves, but God calls us to a deeper love than what we can give ourselves. This love is not a twisted version of the real story like the fairytale; it's the highest form of self-care: letting God love us enough to change us, rescue us, heal us, and restore us to Himself. The real Hero of our life's story actually looks like a King who came to conquer what is broken and to redeem what is His.

We are about to crack open the pages of this story together to reveal the "happily ever after" that is everything we are searching for and so much more.

3 THE MESSAGES

What does the fairytale sound like?

I'm one of those people with irrational fear. Well, just one big fear specifically. It's called ichthyophobia, and it sounds pretty legitimate until you realize that ichthyophobia is the fear of fish. I am afraid of looking at fish and especially being in the water with them. I have no problem eating fish or sushi though. Explain that one. People ask where this fear came from, and the only memory that comes to mind was when I visited an aquarium at the age of 10 and a large fish swam by, making eye contact with me in the most spine-chilling way. We had a staring contest, and I did not win.

When my husband and I were on our honeymoon in Aruba, we both determined that I would get into the water. How could you vacation in Aruba and never get in the water? My poor, brand new husband, snorkeled solo while I sat on the beach. Until one of the days where he invited me into the water, and I decided to be brave and get in— more so just to say that I did.

The warm water washed over my feet. I was doing it. I took a few more steps in, my eyes carving out a path around me to ensure that I would not have any scaly visitors. I splashed the water a lot because I knew that scared fish. People around us probably had a lot of questions about the scene that was unfolding.

My husband handed me his goggles and told me to dip my face in the water because there was a fish a long way off that he wanted me to see as a "warm-up," a way to get used to being in the water. I made him promise me that it was far enough away that I would have a couple of seconds to run out of the water if need be. He nodded. With my head in the water only enough to see the fish, I spotted the fish a ways off. It wasn't as exciting to me like it was to him, but nonetheless, I pulled my head out of the water and congratulated myself for a big win. That wasn't so bad.

Within a few minutes, I threw all caution to the wind and found myself about waist-deep in the water. Kicking and splashing to create a safe space around me, my husband, who had continued his shallow-water snorkeling, invited me to get on his back for safety. What a guy. I'm sure he wasn't embarrassed at all at the scene of my flailing, keep-the-fish-away body in the calm and crystal clear blue waters. He handed me the goggles a second time and told me to put my face in the water again. This time, he gave no warning of what I was going to be looking for, but I trusted him and my flailing methods enough to not ask questions.

I took a deep breath, pushed the goggles on tight, and lowered my head into the water. Within one moment, I found myself in the middle of one of my greatest nightmares. We were entirely surrounded by a school of fish. Not just hundreds or thousands, but millions. (Ok, maybe thousands, but my memory says millions.) I flung my head up and out of the water, dug my claws into his shoulders, and began kicking my legs around to make sure not one of those little guys touched me, not even for a second. Like a water-flying scene from Jaws, but without an ounce of blood. I whispered in his ear, "PLEASE GET ME OUT OF THIS WATER RIGHT NOW WITHOUT MAKING A SCENE!" As if people were going to think that he was the crazy one.

In case you're wondering, yes, we are still happily married, but I haven't gone into the ocean with him and a pair of goggles since.

Something Far More Dangerous

The ocean, in all of its vastness, has a lot of creatures and depths of unknown and unchartered territory, but there is one thing about the ocean that is scarier than fish, sharks, or whatever your water fear may be. Perhaps my fear of fish is irrational, but there is another ocean danger that is rational to fear. One of the greatest dangers in the ocean for humans is a rip current.

The rip current occurs on the surface of the water and is a strong and narrow flow of water that runs from shore out to sea. It often can flow faster than an Olympic swimmer, and if people get swept into the current, they can find themselves out in deeper waters very quickly. Rip currents never flow toward the shore, only out to the open sea. A person cannot swim against them because they will wear her out to the point of exhaustion as it only flows in one direction, and the shoreline gets smaller as one is swept away from the beach. Many people every year have to be rescued from rip currents, while others lose their lives in the fight against the current once they've been swept far away from shore. The average person would not be able to identify the rip current just by looking at the water, which is why so many people get caught in them without realizing it. A beautiful day's swim can quickly turn into a nightmare.

There is a rip current that is flowing through our culture. The world around us has created its own ideas of what it looks like to really be happy and to find worth and identity in ourselves. The ocean waters of our culture are irresistible. They represent our insatiable desire to understand our life's purpose, to find our significance, and to leave a mark. We spend a lot of time in the ocean of culture, working hard to make a difference in our world, meanwhile, the rip current flows unseen as we are drawn deeper into the ocean. First, the water splashes against our knees in our curiosity, then it rises to our waist as we explore, and eventually, we're up to our neck in full commitment. Our feet can no longer feel the shifting sand in between our toes as we drift further into the self-discovery journey.

We're convinced that whatever is broken about us can also be fixed by us if we choose to put ourselves first and start doing the work of self-care and healing on our own, apart from God. The messaging and language of influencers on social media, celebrities, beauty, and fashion brands, is one that has now trickled all the way down to our children, inviting all of us into an unseen pathway of water that only moves one way. What's most concerning is not that the rip current of self-discovery to self-love exists, but that we are now so used to it that we hit the like button and keep on scrolling. We are jumping into the current without realizing its power or its ultimate destination: away from home and away from God. The possibility of danger in the water no longer phases us. Honestly, we can't get into the water fast enough.

The rip current of the fairytale begins with hand-crafted messages. These messages are words of hope and beacons of light to a worn-out mom or a college student under a lot of stress. The fairytale story always begins with these messages. Women, we love words that we can hold onto, that we can trust and lean on. Words like "positivity," "empowerment," "strong enough," "deserve," and "self-love." We want to know that we are enough, that we are capable, that we matter, and that we are loved no matter what we look like or feel like. As a desperate college student who hated her body, I would have wrapped these words tightly around myself as anchors for my restless and weary soul. That's why I know the fairytale personally, the strength of the current. It's also why I carry the burden of the importance of exposing the rip current of our culture's self-first messaging. An innocent swim too close to the current doesn't come without a great and expensive price.

How can you identify the rip current? What gives it away? Most of the time, keywords (as mentioned only a few sentences ago) and phrases, that we will now unpack together, expose it. Word of caution (and excitement!): you are now entering the I-know-too-much-to-ignore-the-truth zone.

"I deserve to be happy, healthy, whole…"

The pain hit me out of nowhere. But, this wasn't an unfamiliar pain unfortunately. I knew this pain pretty well by now. Each time it hit me, it felt like a bolt of lightning crawling up my neck and into my eye. My ears rang in an agonizing tone as I wiggled my head into my pillow, praying that I could find an ounce of relief in the soft, cotton cloud. The pain amplified by ten. Please, no. I can't do this again, I would think to myself. I dreaded the pain, this unwelcomed visitor. With every migraine, I only had about 15-20 minutes before the situation would intensify, so I needed to settle into bed quickly. Waves of nausea would roll over me, one after another, some forcing me to jump out of bed so I wouldn't throw up all over my sacred space. I didn't know what was going on in the world around me. I could hear my girls playing, but I felt like a world away from them. Underneath the melting and dripping ice pack that I kept wrapped around my head, the pain silenced my thoughts and ability to engage with anyone around me. There is nothing worse than being a mom who is experiencing a physical barrier of pain keeping her from her children. I couldn't fake a smile through it. I couldn't escape for a moment and pull myself together. These days were physically painful, but also emotionally devastating—I was captive to the pain while my family helplessly witnessed its hold over me.

The truth was that for three years right after my youngest daughter, Willow, was born I dealt with these crippling migraines, sometimes up to a dozen per month. At one point, I didn't think that I would be able to find a job and work because of the nature and frequency of my migraines.

My husband and I had our own language or sign when it came to these days. All I had to do was look at him a certain way, or tell him that I'd be in bed and he knew that I was going to be down for the day. My migraines felt like true suffering. I've delivered two children naturally without any pain medication—both of which took me to the point of pain like I was knocking on death's door. In fact, I didn't know that I couldn't get an epidural for my first daughter's birth until I was halfway through my labor. I'm pretty sure I spent a good portion of that delivery begging the doctor to "save me," but I'll leave that story for another time. My migraines felt like another form of torture. So, when the migraine would subside, I found myself thinking about how grateful I was to be alive. Post-migraine, I felt like I could conquer the world. Everything tasted better, smelled better, sounded better…it was like a black and white movie coming back into full color.

"You deserve happiness, health, and healing" was a phrase that a friend of mine said to me as we discussed my debilitating migraines. I deserved to be happy, I deserved healing, and I deserved peace. I didn't deserve to suffer, right? Was I unaware of a big mistake in my life? I wouldn't wish these migraines on my worst enemy.

The words, "You deserve happiness, health, and healing" cut past my outer layers and spoke directly to my heart. The fairytale was inviting me into the big, wide world of possibilities. I really wanted to believe this for my life. Didn't I deserve to be healthy? My family didn't deserve these migraines to steal me away from them. I didn't deserve to suffer in front of my children and miss out on a lot of perfectly good days with them. They didn't deserve to see mom like that.

The "I deserve it" belief lives in the rip current. Our culture's self-care model is built on the fairytale story that we deserve to live life without disruption to our peace, our happiness, or our wellbeing. But, how can we fully control a peace that we didn't create in the first place? 1 Corinthians 14:33 says, "*For God is not the author of confusion but of peace, as in all the churches of the saints.*" To know real peace, we have to get it from the Source. A broken world and imperfect humanity will always yield brokenness. We may desire a peace-filled life, but Jesus didn't die for our peace; He died for our souls. What we truly deserve in this life is not peace, but death and separation from God. But in His goodness, Jesus covered the cost by His own body and blood. Once we realize that everything; every breath, every sunrise, every second is a gift from our Creator, only then we will feel differently about the "I deserve it" mantra.

As we receive peace and joy through Christ, we find more than any amount we could achieve on our own and we experience them in their fullest amount: filled to the brim and overflowing.

And, as Christian women, we have to start being phased by the messaging around us. It needs to alert our senses and cause us to pause. We have to dissect it before we accept it. We have to rub the sleepiness from our eyes to see the self-love messaging that is infiltrating our world because it all eventually leads to the heart. We are eating up the words of the world faster than we can chew. We are allowing the self-love messaging to come pouring out of our lips as we declare our undying love to ourselves in front of the world—because the world instructs us to.

But the words of culture and the words of Jesus are not working together for your good. At large, they are in constant opposition to each other. The words, phrases, thoughts, and ideas of culture are not words of darkness and slander and evil. No, the reason that we find ourselves in the current is that we were captivated first by the beauty of the ocean, or the vastness of finding our purpose and significance, without realizing there is a rip current of self underneath all of it. The messaging of self-love all around us sounds beautiful. It speaks of light and life and love—just like Jesus taught. But, it's not at all the same light, life, or love. This is where the danger comes in; the light and life and love of the world don't begin or end with Jesus. These begin and end with self.

Why do we have a hard time distinguishing between the world's message and the truth? Culture preaches a self-love message that values life, not death. It teaches the availability of hope and peace and worth. And if we, as Christians, are not grounded in the Word of God and walk in a vibrant relationship with Him, we will not be able to tell the difference between messaging that sounds the same as Jesus' words but worships an entirely different god—the god of self.

The "god of self" messaging is here and is so ingrained that we hardly even notice it. It's packaged so beautifully and in a way that seems to undeniably make the most sense. If we want to know the world around us, we have to know ourselves, right? If we want to fully love ourselves, we have to go on a journey to discover who we are and what we have to offer the world. We have to uncover all of our brokenness and study it closely. We must fill our time learning how to be ok with our brokenness and how to begin healing ourselves.

The messaging and marketing of our current culture is like the rip current, hardly noticeable, but quick to set your heart and mind on a new path away from shore and away from home. In order to spot them, you have to know what they sound like. Here are just a few examples of the positive messages that can draw you into the self-discovery current:

- **Manifest anything that you want in life, and you'll receive it.**
- **Own your truth.**
- **You won't begin to heal until you begin to know yourself.**
- **You have to start the heart work yourself.**
- **Learn to be selfish to protect your peace.**
- **Healing comes from the inside.**
- **Just be the real you, unapologetically!**
- **How you feel matters more than what they think.**
- **Nothing matters more than your happiness and peace.**
- **You've got one life—do what is most important to you.**
- **Be the energy that you hope to attract.**

You may read this list and nod your head in agreement, or you may also read this list and feel personally attacked. How could the words in this list be wrong? Can they really do any harm at all? Isn't a person just staying in her own lane and minding her own business and well-being when she says things like this? Why should it matter to anyone else if she says these things? Lean into the offense. Let God work where you may be stuck.

Each phrase seems so simple, but is instead, wildly complex and disguised, like the wolf who dressed up as Grammy in Little Red Riding Hood. He was her enemy disguised as the grandmother that she loved. He wanted to eat her, not feed her.

He went to a familiar location, Grammy's house, and made himself at home. That is the work of our enemy: to enter our world and to make lies look believable and achievable. All in an effort to destroy us.

These self-empowerment phrases have two things in common: self + control. The world is fooling us with self-promotion disguised as positivity. Do you see it? The illusion and rip current of these phrases is that they aren't inherently wrong or bad. But they are lacking the most important factor: Creator God.

Christine Caine, author, speaker, and founder of A21 ministries has said, "The only love language is 'die to self.'" If someone you know or admire is giving you advice that leads you back to yourself to find answers, confirmation, affirmation, or healing, then let that be your giant red flag. If a celebrity or brand that you love is delivering this type of advice through advertising or otherwise, remember that they are not the authority on this matter. They may seem authentic and genuine in their pursuit of happiness in inclusivity, but they did not create you. They did not plan out your life before you were ever even a thought. They do not know you or care about your deepest hurts and hang-ups. Only God does. We have to stop confusing the two.

2 Corinthians 11:14 says "...*for even Satan disguises himself as an angel of light.*" What we know is that the father of evil can look like an angel of light, confusing and drawing in anyone who is looking for light apart from God Himself. Just because something or someone draws you into a message of hope doesn't mean that it is the message of light and hope. Apart from God, there is nothing truly good.

The One-Degree Shift

Self-love messaging is used all of the time as a way to encourage, uplift, and empower ourselves and other people. Women say these things to other women all of the time. So often, in fact, that I hear Christian women using these phrases in partnership with spiritual encouragement. As if God had left it out of the Bible on accident. You may still be wondering, but why is it a problem for us to say these kinds of things to each other or to ourselves? If you are a Jesus-follower, sometimes the most dangerous roads we take aren't in the complete opposite direction of God. We don't always make blatantly wrong and sinful choices that leave us feeling distant from God. In many cases, just like this one, it's a simple one-degree shift that sets us in a direction that will eventually lead us completely off course. Put plainly, a one-degree shift can change our entire journey.

My dad is a pilot. He had his pilot's license before he had his driver's license because, from a very young age, he knew that was what he wanted to fly planes every day. When we were little, my dad would take us to the hangar of the private corporation for which he worked. We could go into the parked airplanes and see his office space and we always got some gum that the pilots kept in the cockpit. As little kids that was the highlight of being inside of a private jet, the gum. I remember my dad telling me about this rule of thumb that pilots have called the "1 in 60" rule. It means that if you become just one degree off course at any point in the flight, you will miss your destination by 1 mile for every 60 miles that you fly. One degree off course can change your entire destination. Setting a journey off course is never done on purpose. The factors that can put a plane so far off course include the wind, poor planning, distractions, and more.

The steps that put us onto the self-first journey, leading to life completely independent from God, are rarely taken on purpose. Like wind patterns that push a plane, our life experiences leave us within the tension of whether to trust ourselves or to trust God with the restoration from hurt and trauma. We can't deny or ignore the things that we've experienced. As a plane can't fly without the impact of the wind, so we can't ignore the factors of our past that will always exist and leave us vulnerable to small decisions of placing our hope and trust in the wrong person. Too many self-care days and Netflix binges only leave us more broken in our trauma because numbing out to reality leaves no room for God to heal the physical and emotional parts of us.

To avoid the one-degree shift, we have to acknowledge our past and make God our first point of contact for healing. With the understanding that our life experiences impact our mental health, we will take a deeper dive into mental health in the coming chapters. Our course is impacted by our past, but it doesn't have to be changed by our past. If we are diligent to seek God first, we will quickly find ourselves back on track.

Poor planning, another avoidable one-degree shift, happens when we don't leave enough room for clarity of thought. Like a pilot who is in a hurry, or who is climbing into the cockpit exhausted from life, mistakes can easily happen. "Fatigue science" exists within the Federal Aviation Administration, which has concluded that all pilots must have eight consecutive hours of sleep with an additional two hours of rest for a total of ten hours, every twenty-four hours, before every flight. Why? Because poor planning can cause physical death, but it can also cause spiritual death if we end up with a life that is all about ourselves, and not at all about God. With our busy lives, running at high speeds with little rest, poor planning happens often and even without us noticing. We don't plan for quiet moments with God. We don't plan to praise Him or to pray and fast over life's decisions. We don't plan to run to Him first when our parents get sick or when our children struggle. We don't plan to go to God when anxiety and depression strike and life becomes too overwhelming. Poor planning leaves the door wide open for us to lean on our own understanding and feelings when we are burdened by life. One small choice to take control of today's plan can lead to a one-degree shift off course toward a self-reliant life if we don't catch it soon enough.

In 1987, Northwest flight 255 took off in Detroit, Michigan just 15 minutes from my house, and crashed within minutes of takeoff, killing all but one little girl on board. My dad had just talked to one of the passengers that morning at church. It shook the community to its core and we still talk about it almost every time we drive to the airport together. The cause of the crash was later revealed that the pilots failed to thoroughly check off the taxi checklist and they missed the extension of the flaps and slats for takeoff. They were distracted. Possibly in a hurry or possibly just tired.

We've never been more distracted. The world sends millions of messages that distract us, messages encouraging us to live our lives to honor ourselves instead of God. Messages that encourage us to live self-obsessed by showing us all of the things that other people are doing, leaving us with massive guilt trips and longing for better lives. These messages distract us because they are shiny and positive, and they feel relevant to our goals of to loving ourselves and enjoying our lives. One self-love message here may not seem to hurt anything, but it only takes one to cause us to accept the next one, and the next, and the next. One self-love message that we accept as good or as truth is a one-degree shift to an entire journey off course. When it comes to the words and beliefs that we are allowing into our hearts and minds, it doesn't take deliberately wrong choices. The errors are subtle, and today, it can simply start out with the sound of an empowering message of self-love.

The Voice of the Fairytale

"Own your truth and live in it"

Owning your truth is a way of saying, "stop conforming." Owning your truth and living in it simply means being true to yourself. It's not a bad start, right? Living your truth means making decisions that honor your own self as the top priority of your life. It means dressing how you feel comfortable dressing, not how society expects you to dress. It means not involving yourself in things or people that could potentially disturb your inner peace or comfort.

Truth is not subjective. John 14:6, *"Jesus said to him, 'I am the way, and the truth, and the life. No one comes to the Father except through me.'"* Jesus didn't say that He was the truth as one option of many for truth. Jesus said this because He is also Creator God Who established truth long before He put breath into the first human. Truth has an origin, and the origin is God, not us. Whatever God says about truth is true. John 8:23 says, *"And you will know the truth, and the truth will set you free."* The truth is meant to be known, not created on an individual basis. The truth is meant to be followed.

The freedom of owning truth comes when we live with The Truth, God Himself. In God, we find beautiful individuality, unexplainable inner peace, and answers to all of life's questions. A self-discovery to find our own truth will only get us so far. In fact, God as Truth incites a different reaction than self-love. In Exodus 3:6, Moses hid his face in fear when God spoke to him. When Isaiah saw God, he cried, *"Woe to me! I am ruined! For I am a man of unclean lips, and I live among a people of unclean lips"* (6:5). In Luke 5:8, Peter saw Jesus and said, *"Go away from me Lord, I'm a sinful man!"* Revelation 1:17 says, *"When I saw Him, I fell at His feet as though dead. Then He placed His right hand on me and said: 'Do not be afraid. I am the First and the Last.'"* People who encountered God did not fall more in love with themselves. They rejected who they were in light of God and knew they needed the Truth of God to change every part of them. These people wouldn't have considered creating their own truth in the presence of God. Truth was right in front of them. He defined Truth, He gave the truth, and they just had to accept it in order to find the freedom they so desperately wanted.

When we encounter God, we realize our sin is incompatible with a perfect and holy God. When we encounter God, we realize that there is nothing that we can do for ourselves that would ever compare to what God has available for us. Many women are headed on a journey to find their own truth in order to own the very thing that God offers through Himself. If the few people in Scripture who experienced the presence of God could not stand His physical glory, and if truth is found in the glory of God, then may I suggest that the truth isn't something we can own, but that the Truth, instead, owns us? Isaiah 43:1 says, *"But now, this is what the LORD says— he who created you, Jacob, he who formed you, Israel: "Do not fear, for I have redeemed you; I have summoned you by name; you are mine."* We, then, should turn "own your truth" to "follow The Truth."

"Healing Starts from Within"

We can start with Jesus and begin using language like the phrases that I listed, not seeing any difference in how that language can turn into beliefs that can then interfere with the work that Jesus is trying to do in us—which is to make us look more like Him and less like us. A one-degree shift that sounds like, "I have to figure out how to heal this part of myself" leads to believing and acting on the idea that "healing comes from the inside." Without further examination or running that idea through Scripture, the temptation is to believe what the world has said, that the healing starts and ends with you alone, while Jesus says, yes, healing happens in you, but through Him alone. Psalm 147:3 says, *"He heals the brokenhearted and binds up their wounds."*

"The Ultimate Goal is to Be at Peace with Yourself"

I would argue that aside from love, peace is a close second at the top of every person's priority list. People ache to find peace within themselves. But real peace is not something that we can earn or work to achieve. I can find peace in the quiet of my house when my kids are in school, yes. I can find peace momentarily with myself when I'm not at odds with anyone or anything in my life. I can find peace when I understand that my past has no hold on me and what my future holds. But that's not real peace at all. That is circumstantial peace, peace that is a result of "getting to the other side" of whatever disrupted our peace.

Real peace is not finally feeling good about yourself, but finding an Anchor apart from self. The world says that the anchor is you. God says that the Anchor can only be Him. Real peace feels like an anchor like you're secured to something safe and trustworthy. But it's even more than that.

Real, God-given peace, which is not something we can create on our own self-discovery journey, is actually anchored to the Hope of this life and the freedom of Life in the next! Real peace is not a lack of chaos; it's the filling of unconditional love, unwavering stability, overwhelming hope, and an eternity with Jesus to which you can look forward. Hebrews 6 is the hype passage for peace in scripture:

> *So when God desired to show more convincingly to the heirs of the promise the unchangeable character of his purpose, he guaranteed it with an oath, so that by two unchangeable things [God's promise + God's oath], in which it is impossible for God to lie, we who have fled for refuge might have strong encouragement to hold fast to the hope set before us. We have this as a sure and steadfast anchor of the soul, a hope that enters into the inner place behind the curtain, 20 where Jesus has gone as a forerunner on our behalf, having become a high priest forever after the order of Melchizedek. (v. 17–19)*

Our Anchor is firm but unseen. It's not something we have to create in ourselves or discover as a hidden treasure. It's a peace that is an anchor for our soul and hope that comes from a place where, in our humanity, we were/are incapable to go on our own, "into the inner place behind the curtain." Only Jesus. Only Jesus as a forerunner on our behalf. I love the word "forerunner" because, in Greek, the word is "prodromos" which was the word for "reconnaissance man." In military terms, this was the man who would run ahead of everyone to scout out and defeat the enemy. This man would run knowing that others would follow him. While the world tells you to muster up peace by figuring yourself out, Scripture shows us that Jesus, who is our peace, paid a debt that we couldn't pay on the cross, went to the depths of death and despair that we were condemned to experience without Him, and then continuously runs toward our enemy declaring the victory that we are covered in His blood and anchored in His love. The world is doing its best to lead you away from this and back to yourself. Fight to know Jesus. He fought death to have you.

Frost, Rob. 2001. A Closer Look at New Age Spirituality. Eastbourne: Kingsway.

Christian women: Train your eyes and ears to see and hear the self-discovery messaging. Evaluate what is being said. Who is the focal point of the phrase? Who does this put in control of the outcome? You or God?

Are you going to be the hero of your own story? The goal of the fairytale is to shape and mold the lead character to come to the conclusion that she doesn't need anyone other than herself. When you know Christ, this is not your story. This is not your happily ever after.

Consider the cost when we, having the hope and light of Jesus, give any kind of false hope to self-reliance or inner strength that seems more powerful than the work of God Himself? Pause to evaluate the message you are sharing. Help women discover the power of Jesus that outperforms the power they have in themselves. Point women to the One who loves them more than they could ever dream to love themselves. Don't let women in your life live by the belief that they are "good enough" when they are more than enough because of Jesus in them.

To women who are seeking wholeness: the messages that you see and hear all around you, encouraging you to look inside of yourself for all of the answers and strength, have no connection to eternity, only to the limited details of today. Light and positivity and all that the fairytale promises are mere illusions without the power of Jesus. Control and independence do not lead to peace, because we are incapable of controlling our life entirely. Our messy life happened to us because of broken people and as a result of mistakes we've made. A world of people who come from the same brokenness are the very ones telling us to keep looking inward to find the answers. So be wise, because all paths and pursuits of "peace" that are void of God, the Creator, and Healer of our souls, lead to the same place: a lifetime and eternity separated from Him and all good things.

But God makes big promises that we can accept as our truth because it is the truth that we were created to know. It's the truth that sets us fully and entirely free:

God says He makes us **strong**: *"God arms me with strength, and he makes my way perfect"* (Psalm 18:32).

God says He makes us **whole**: *"So you also are complete through your union with Christ, who is the head over every ruler and authority"* (Colossians 2:10).

God says He **gives us direction:** *"Whether you turn to the right or to the left, your ears will hear a voice behind you, saying 'This is the way; walk in it'"* (Isaiah 30:21).

God says you are **powerful, loved, and have a sound mind:** *"For God hath not given us the spirit of fear, but of power, and of love, and of a sound mind"* (2 Timothy 1:7).

He waits for you. He longs to rescue you, to pick you up and give you everything that you need. The very last thing that you were designed to be was an independent woman. You were knit together in your mother's womb in God's image so that you would know and depend on Him. He's waiting to pour His love out on you, and as it fills every crack and corner, you will know true love and wholeness for the very first time.

4 THE FAIRYTALE

The fairytale that promises freedom through deeper inner work isn't a thing of the past, and it isn't a phase. The roots of the fairytale are growing deeper with each passing day:

"Originally perceived by many people as a passing fashion, the holistic and New Age movement can no longer be ignored. It threatens established religion, it's activists and thinkers have increasing credibility; it represents the cutting edge of much science, medicine, and psychology; it is a daily feature of contemporary media; and no matter how the establishment intelligentsia may judge it, millions of people are turning to it."

To understand the self-obsessed messaging that has bubbled to the top of our current culture, we have to take an honest look at what's happening now and where it came from. Every belief system has roots.[4]

We've looked at the origin of sin in the Garden of Eden, but now we have to look at how our culture, within the last 70 years, has set the course for today's fairytale. We have to be willing to go there, because, for too long, Christians and unbelievers at large have both called New Age practices crazy non-sense or "weird." We can't ignore the few people who seem to take spirituality "too far" anymore, because those few have turned into massive groups of people who are now teaching their own version of spirituality in a bite-size, palatable way that draws in even the most committed Christians.

Partridge, Christopher. 2006. The Re-Enchantment of the West : Alternative Spiritualities, Sacralization, Popular Culture, and Occulture. London ; New York: T & T Clark International.

The rule of "new spirituality" goes something like this: if it (religion, passed-down beliefs, traditional morality) doesn't work for you, create something that does.

Women are taking things into their own hands. Think about the last time that something in your life wasn't working. What did you do to create a new thing, habit, relationship, escape, or love? If your current gym isn't helping you get results, you switch. If your current friendship isn't working, you find a new friend. If your deodorant isn't doing the job, you find one that does. If the church you've been attending no longer fits your preference, your political beliefs, or your expectations, you switch. Our commitment levels are waning while our preferences and expectations are evolving to better meet our needs. New Spirituality says to find the thing that serves you most. When it no longer serves you, leave it.

I'll let Rob Frost, a respected British Evangelist and author of *A Closer Look at New Age Spirituality* speak for the Christians who are feeling the strongest pull of the New Age movement:

"To be frank", he confesses, "I am deeply disillusioned with what the church is offering Sunday by Sunday. There is a deadness in the ritual, a dryness in the formality, and a growing irrelevance in the institution … I find a genuine hunger for spiritual things in the New Age community, an openness to try new ideas, and a deep respect for the beliefs of others … I share the hunger for the fulfilling kind of spirituality which is driving this New Age movement into the mainstream of our culture." Hence, he has become a "spiritual searcher" and invites his fellow Christians to follow him as he wanders "around the supermarket of ideas of New Age culture, [in order to] see what they can teach [him] about [his] own quest for deep spirituality." As he says, "I am becoming a New Age Christian, and I am not alone. Many committed Christians are looking for something deeper in their everyday life and faith."[5]

We are shifting to be more "spiritual but not religious." To simplify, religion means following a specific belief system while spirituality means following your heart and what feels

[5] Partridge, Christopher H. 2004. The Re-Enchantment of the West. Vol. I : Alternative Spiritualities, Sacralization, Popular Culture and Occulture. London: T & T Clark International.

best to you. People may refer to Christians as being very "spiritual," meaning that they are in daily communication with the Holy Spirit and live in obedience to Him. However, today, more than ever, spirituality is culture's buzzword and has little to nothing to do with God the Creator and everything to do with our inner selves, our inner work, and an earth and universe where God isn't central. When we talk about spirituality, we are rarely talking about the Holy Spirit and His work in our lives. I hear the word "spirituality" thrown around in Christian circles a lot. It is confusing for new believers and even life-long Christ-followers because, as we will discuss in the coming chapter, culture's version of spirituality is drastically different. It promises light, love, and life, just like Jesus promises through Himself. But culture's spirituality and Jesus don't mix, and they certainly do not match. Cultural, man-made spirituality is void of the True God, leaving the space wide open for us to become our own gods within time and space:

"Mystical impulse emerges, driven by internalization of religion. Interior personal experience replaces exterior doctrine and ethics. Fellowships or networks of "experiencers" form to share ideas, but they lack the organization and structure of the worship-oriented sect. Indeed, Troeltsch indicates that, because of the lack of centralized structure, such mystical religion becomes eclectic, incorporating new ideas, and a luxury principally available to, and appealing to, the educated middle classes. Again, this epistemological individualism, of course, comes very close to what we would now describe as "New Age" spirituality." [3]

This Mysticism isn't new. We see mystical religion happening in Acts 17 when Paul visited Athens. He met with a group of Stoic and Epicurean philosophers. Stoics were pantheists (we will cover pantheism in this chapter). They believed that everything was god and that god was in everything. These well-educated and hungry for knowledge people believed that there was no particular destiny for mankind, establishing the belief that nothing in life should be resisted. Epicureans were also hungry for knowledge and open to hearing every belief and religion. They pursued pleasure, peace, and painlessness as their chief purpose in life. Paul stoked their ego saying, "*I see that in every way you are very religious!*" (verse 22) Going on, Paul points out the sinkhole in their worldview: "*For as I walked around and looked carefully at your objects of worship, I even found an altar with this inscription: TO AN UNKNOWN GOD. So you are ignorant of the very thing you worship...*"

Freedom to worship anything or anyone that you want comes with a price: a journey without a destination and a life without truth.

Pick and Choose Spirituality

My husband, Colston, has been a pastor of some kind (youth, discipleship, small groups, campus) for the last 13 years. We've heard a consistent concern from men and women that we've talked to about coming to our church or any church: committing to a religion feels like a life-altering decision because, if you join a church, you accept all of its beliefs and practices. In love, we have to shift the conversation to help them see that Jesus wasn't religious, but instead, obedient to the Father, and we are expected to be the same. For those who don't follow Jesus, religion can be too much of a commitment. Not a single religion checks all of their feelings, beliefs, or political views perfectly, so why commit to one? Spirituality opens up endless possibilities for the non-committal soul. Ironically, more options don't lead to peace, but to confusion and restlessness.

Choosing a life of spirituality gives women the flexibility to pick and choose what practices work for them. This "pick and choose" approach to spirituality means that we may or not be as "extreme" to read tarot cards or use crystals or study astrology, but we may still choose to live with a spiritual mantra on our lips such as "I love myself" or "I am ready to be seen" or "I am powerful and independent."

The fairytale is rooted in New-Age thinking and terminology that is gripping women and Christian women more now than ever before. How have the New Age beliefs become so prevalent, even inside of Christian circles? "Before the internet, people who held beliefs outside the mainstream — religious, political or otherwise — lacked a public way to connect with one another. With social media, she said, divinatory practices like astrology, crystals, and tarot have been able to take up space in a public conversation. It helps that they all look great on Instagram." [5]

Social media is a breeding ground for a new level of spirituality, and most women are showing up for it, whether they realize it or not. The lure of awakening our best inner selves isn't a Gen Z or Millennial thing. New Age beliefs have been around in this country for a long time, and the baseline of their belief system has been around since the garden. The core belief and message is this: you get to be god.

As we watch New Age beliefs picking up steam in our culture, I want to remind you that while the appeal of the fairytale may seem like it offers a deep ocean of possibilities, its impact is, in fact, extremely shallow.

"Not only does New Age spirituality have little impact upon the world, it also has a negligible effect on the lives of the individual believers." Bruce says, "It allows novices to become adepts without the difficult bits in between … What is advertised as spiritual transformation is little more than acquiring a new vocabulary." Unlike Methodism, which transformed the lives of individuals who then went on to transform the societies in which they lived, the New Age does neither. [6]

Jessica Roy. "Must-Reads: How Millennials Replaced Religion with Astrology and Crystals." Los Angeles Times. July 10, 2019. https://www.latimes.com/health/la-ne-millennials-religion-zodiac-tarot-crystals-astrology-20190710-story.html.
Partridge, Christopher H. 2004. The Re-Enchantment of the West. Vol. I : Alternative Spiritualities, Sacralization, Popular Culture and Occulture. London: T & T Clark International.

Despite what it may look like on a beautiful social media post with a woman sitting outside in nature, a person cannot impact on the world when she is consumed with work only for herself. Let's refuse to be deceived. Being able to recognize New Age thinking today is critical to avoiding its snare. Satan is working hard to encourage doubt in our minds. Is God the only way? Is spirituality really dangerous? Is Emily over-spiritualizing something that is harmless? In order to answer those questions, we must uncover the roots of the fairytale. What's lurking underneath the surface?

When Mental Health and New Age Culture Collide

Before we dig up the New Age roots of the fairytale lying beneath the surface, it's critical to address a major issue that directly impacts the fairytale and has disrupted people's lives in so many ways: breakdowns in mental health. Why is it important to talk about mental health in the same space where we are talking about New Age beliefs? Because for Christ-followers and non-Christ-followers, mental health issues are driving us inward.

Hear me when I say this: if you struggle with anxiety, depression, or any other mental health issue, you are not broken beyond repair. You are not beyond God's realm of healing and wholeness. You are not a project that must be picked apart and analyzed to death. You are made in the image of God and fully eligible for healing. If God only used "whole" people, He would have shut down this whole human thing a long time ago. He wants to partner with us in our frailness. We get to do the work with God without the weight of the world on our shoulders (that was Jesus' job). Anxiety and depression are not your identity; they are a part of the human condition.

I dealt with crippling anxiety in my early 20's (which was like yesterday, for the record). I couldn't walk through a crowd without having a panic attack. Anti-anxiety medicines calmed me down, but they also left me feeling like a zombie.

There was no happy medium. My husband and I were working for a church in southern California at the time. We had only been married for a couple of years, so as you can imagine, my husband felt helpless not knowing how to intervene. Our job was serving the church, teaching God's Word, and pointing people to Jesus. But I couldn't pull myself together enough to even be able to endure the normal crowd around me most days. It wasn't a matter of praying more to get past the anxiety. Could God have healed me instantly at any given time? Without a doubt. But, He allowed it, and I believe He allowed it in my life for a couple of reasons: to remind me of Who was actually in control at all times and to create a deeper dependence on Him. If that sounds like spiritual words or Christian talk that you can't understand, please know that I did not come to those conclusions until almost a decade later. God often allows us to walk through difficult seasons without answers. Answers don't equal God's favor by the way. Answers that explain why God allowed things can be helpful, but even if God had stayed silent about my anxiety, He would still be just as worthy and just as in control of my life.

The New Age belief system revolves around one person: you. And with mental health issues as widespread as they are, the two are colliding more than ever before. The message is this: You need to focus only on yourself in order to heal yourself. To be clear, I believe that counseling and therapy is absolutely effective. I believe that God gives us tools and people to partner with us when we are not doing well to help us see what we can't.

The world, operating as if the healing power of God doesn't exist, tells us that we have the strength in and of ourselves alone to find complete healing and wholeness. These are not the words of Jesus. He said that He alone is the way, the truth, and the life—that no one can come to the Father except through Him. If wholeness could be found in ourselves, Jesus' life, ministry, and death were all in vain. We can find help through therapies and counseling that can help us redirect our thoughts and minds. We can treat our bodies well through diet and exercise to aid in our healing. There are steps that we have to take to get better. But if the therapy we seek is not leading us to Jesus as the Healer, in the end, we can only make progress so far. We can only progress within our human limits. Jesus heals us on the soul level.

When dealing with mental health issues, "working on yourself" with a Christ-centered perspective is going to lead you to Jesus. The world's definition of working on yourself will lead you back to you. Partner with Jesus in your healing journey, and let Him fight with you because He's already fought for you...and He'll never stop!

It's vital to know the difference between a Christ-centered perspective in therapy versus a secular perspective on therapy. Without Christ at the center, New Age myths will be introduced to fragile hearts and minds, leaving people more confused than when they arrived. To guard our hearts against unhelpful therapy sessions is to know the enemy's schemes. Don't let the enemy take advantage of your weakness. Combat him with the truth that Jesus is Lord and that He is trustworthy to heal and restore you, with or without therapy, and with or without other lifestyle changes. Let's begin uncovering the truth of what we are up against as we debunk the New Age myths together.

Myth #1: Best Case Scenario: One-ness with Ourselves and the World

In New Age beliefs, "monism" is the goal. Monism is the belief that all is one, all earth, all humanity, all beliefs. New Agers thus stress that all which exists is "consciousness" and that there is a single, unified consciousness. Human beings are part of this consciousness and individuals are fragments of this oneness. (1) Claiming all people, the earth, and all beliefs as one is appealing because it's entirely inclusive. No one gets left out. No one has to feel shame or to feel unwelcome. Believing that everything is one allows people to live comfortably with all of the things that don't make sense going on around them. It's easy to contain a river without any canals or streams. When everyone is headed in the same direction, it gives us a sense of control and power.

Jesus talked about "one-ness," so it's easy for Christian women to be confused why I would say that monism is wrong. He said, "*I in them and you in me, that they may become perfectly one, so that the world may know that you sent me and loved them even as you loved me*" (John 17:23). Jesus is saying that people could be one body in *Him*, not one body apart from Him with millions of different belief systems. Not one body with each individual living for the ultimate happiness and fulfillment of itself. He wanted his followers to be "perfectly one" for one purpose: "'so that the world may know that You sent me and loved them even as You loved me.'" Knowing God, not knowing self is the highest goal.

Jesus was talking about all of humanity, even though He knew that few would actually follow Him. Jesus died for all of humanity, knowing that few would choose Him over themselves. Jesus wasn't only about a few. He was about all. All people follow Him and working with eternity in mind.

So as we work really hard to champion each other as human beings, we have to be careful that we are not championing humanity apart from God, but rather a humanity that is fully united and redeemed by Him and in His Name.

Myth #2: God is Everything

New Age beliefs claim that God is in everything. Sound familiar? Christians believe the same thing, except it's not the same thing at all. Pantheism is the belief that "all is god" and everything is a manifestation of God. That term "all is god" means that everything you see is God and that God is everything, including you and me.

To break it down a little further, Emilie Cady, an American homeopathic physician and author of New Thought spiritual writings says in her book Lessons of Truth, that God is not a being among beings. She claims that God is the ground or a source of being. God is not the source of power and intelligence and knowledge; he exists only as power, or

Cady, Emily H., "Lessons in Truth: A Course of Twelve Lessons in Practical Christianity", Unity School of Christianity. 1919.

intelligence or knowledge. [7] He is an "abstract essence." He is not the Spirit but just a spirit. God is what is found in power and happiness and wisdom. This New Age, pantheistic ultimate being exists of spirit, god, nature, and Self. All as one, all equal in power. "Self" gets a capital "S" here.

Without believing that there is one Creator-God from Whom all life and power flow, we then open up our limited minds to try and make sense of what exists all around us. The belief of pantheism is limited to what is here on earth, eliminating the possibility that there is an eternity created by God and designed for His redeemed creation. And, while the beauty and display of nature go beyond our understanding because it was designed by God to draw us to Himself, not away from Himself, believing that it all exists as god brings little hope for what exists beyond this life.

John 3:6 says that *"Flesh gives birth to flesh, but the Spirit gives birth to Spirit."* We start out as flesh, according to John. We do not bring any divine qualities with us into this world. We cannot conjure up any divine qualities as we are unable to create the divine from our human nature. The easiest frame of thought is that we somehow naturally have the attributes of a divine being, but how can we be divine if we had no control over how we ended up on planet earth? We didn't choose anything about our lives until we were at least toddlers. Only the Spirit, Who is also Creator, can change our soul in its natural human condition from dying and decaying to alive and eternal.

How is pantheism disguised today? We don't have to look far to see this belief system. People who hold this belief will never mention God as the Divine Person or Creator or Trinity. They won't talk badly about Him, but they will certainly deny His existence as the One True God if pressed. They claim the power of life comes from everything around them and especially from within themselves with statements like, "You hold the power," "Everything you need is inside of you," "Look to nature to bring you life and healing," etc. This contrasts with Romans 1:25 which says, *"they exchanged the truth of God for a lie, and worshiped and served the creature rather than the Creator."*

It's essentially the heartbeat of today's marketing, whether it's for makeup, health, and fitness, or food service. The goal is to give people the power, to encourage them to take the reins of their life and purchase the product or service that will make them feel god-like: more beautiful, stronger, ultimately the very best version of themselves. This messaging is everywhere because it's an easy sell. Who doesn't want to feel like the very best version of themselves? Who doesn't want to feel like a god or goddess? Adam and Eve were in paradise, but they were tempted with a message that they could be a higher version of themselves. If they got it wrong when things were perfect, we certainly won't get it right today apart from God's power.

As we pull back the wool, we will see that having the freedom to choose our own god and way to that god, doesn't create a solid foundation for our life, but instead a free-for-all of chaos and instability. Christopher Partridge in the Re-enchantment of the West says,

> As we differ in class, in gender, in age, in regional background, in culture we will have different notions of what works for us and this is reflected in the enormous cafeteria of cultural products from which New Agers select. Hence the popular jibe that New Age spirituality is supermarket spirituality—individuals are encouraged to peruse and select from a bewildering array of spiritual products from crop circles and dolphins to Buddhism and Celtic Christianity.[8]

Myth #3: Human Power is Limitless

If pantheism exists, we're now limitless in our abilities, our love, our power, and our control. If something about us is broken, according to New Age beliefs, we have unlimited power within ourselves to fix it and make ourselves whole again. This independent strength and control over our own life can be labeled self-authority.

Partridge, Christopher H. 2004. The Re-Enchantment of the West. Vol. I : Alternative Spiritualities, Sacralization, Popular Culture and Occulture. London: T T Clark International.

With self-authority comes autonomy, and when human autonomy is paired with a belief that there is no Person or Creator God, the door is wide open for people to believe that we are actually the divine. And when we are divinity, we are limitless. The self-authority message is delivered under the guise that "following" the crowd or the societal norms of today handicaps you from your full potential. Self-authority unlocks human power because it stops depending on other people and puts the power in your hands. In order to achieve true success and freedom in life, we are told that one must rely fully on herself. Most of us have experienced the devastation of authority figures in our lives who are imperfect and therefore untrustworthy. So we determine that we are fully capable of carving our own path and discovering happiness on the journey the more that we rely on our own stories and experiences.

But in Matthew 16:24, *"Jesus told His disciples, 'If anyone would come after me, let him deny himself, take up his cross, and follow me.'"*

Jesus didn't stand quietly on the sidelines of this issue. He addressed it head-on because people around Him, like the Jews, thought that they too could live life limitless in their own power. It's a human-condition default. Jesus didn't just know the names of the men and women following Him, He knew their hearts and their hopes and dreams. Jesus knew that they were hungry for happiness and purpose and power. So He gave them the answer, directly from Creator-God: deny your self-authority and follow Me.

Human power is limited to being a human. God has placed a hunger for the divine inside of each of us. It's why pantheism exists in the first place: knowing that we are not enough on our own, it could make sense to try and assign divinity to something or to everything. We've assigned divinity to earth and rocks and the sun because we know that they exist outside of our realm of understanding. And God's creation is intended to show something transcendent and ultimately spiritual:

What may be known of God is manifest in them for God has shown it to them. For since the creation of the world His invisible attributes are clearly seen, being understood by the things that are made, even His eternal power and Godhead, so that they are without excuse. (Romans 1:19,20)

God created nature to reflect Himself and to bring Him glory. In one of my favorite, yet haunting verses, Jesus is speaking to the religious leaders as He is entering Jerusalem one week before He was killed. The leaders were upset that the people were cheering for and worshipping Jesus as He entered the city. Jesus responded saying, *"'I tell you,"* he replied, *"if they keep quiet, the stones will cry out."* Luke 19:40

God will get the glory one way or another, but He uses His creation to leave us in awe and wonder. His world is majestic, but this world isn't God. Our world and everything in it is God's creation, leaving all of the power in His hands: *"The earth is the Lord's, and everything in it, the world, and all who live in it"* (Psalm 24:1).

Myth #4: Morality is Relative

Without having a clear guide of rules and moral standards, New Agers believe that morality is whatever you want it to be. This is called moral relativism. Under moral relativism, anything goes because it's up to the individual to decide what she wants to do. Whether it has a positive or negative impact makes no difference, because a moral compass doesn't exist.

Most people today accept moral objectivism, which means that there are innate rights and wrongs, but there is still room for people to hold their own opinions on what is right and what is wrong. If you accept moral objectivism, you must assume that there is a God or "higher power" that has established the rights and wrongs. For example, most people would agree that sex trafficking is wrong and want to help put an end to it and put its perpetrators behind bars. We were born with this reflex, so it must come from something built into us.

Many influencers and leaders on social media preach the message that you can do anything that feels right to you, no matter what anyone else thinks or how they feel. You get to set the moral compass in your own life. And what is the true north? Whatever makes you happy and whatever sets you "at peace" with yourself. Choices are self-expression.

If we try to stifle someone's self-expression then we become guilty of intolerance. Those who preach moral relativism do so with a goal of total tolerance, hoping to bring unity for all people no matter the cost. The problem with this thinking is that in order to be tolerant, you have to tolerate even those who are intolerant.

In the end, truth and morality are tossed up and thrown around and changed as often as one feels necessary. Most New Age believers would claim that there is no absolute truth, and as someone close to me recently said, you can offer rebuttal to that statement with one question: "Is that absolutely true?"

In Psalm 119:92, David says, *"If Your law had not been my delight, I would have perished in my affliction."* David experienced failures and sufferings in his life. He also experienced the highest levels of power and acceptance. And in all of it, he says that God's law, His moral compass, had been his rescue. God has set morality in place out of His mercy for us, a broken and lost people. As people work to create their own version of morality and tolerance, we can stand in the truth that God isn't tolerant. He is better than that; He is Love.

Myth #5: Culture Believes in Salvation Too

Today, people believe that they can have "salvation" and also have claim an individual consciousness. Not to be confused with the "consciousness" we discussed earlier in this chapter when speaking about the belief that all earth, nature, and humanity are one. This individual consciousness is your awareness of yourself and the world around you. Instead of separating salvation and individual consciousness, they've combined them and then taken Jesus out of the equation altogether. It's important that we discuss this though, because well-intended Christian women often don't realize that salvation is being used in culture less to describe the Gospel and more to describe a transformation of self.

The individual consciousness is an awakening to self. It's a higher state of awareness that is delivered as a pathway to freedom. From a biblical perspective, human consciousness is an awareness of the soul and the world that exists all around it. But individual consciousness and biblical human consciousness are far from the same thing.

In fact, Scripture tells us that, when the Holy Spirit gives consciousness, our soul longs for its Creator and is aware of its own sin and brokenness in comparison to God's holiness. God makes it clear in His word that we are not created to live individually, but with Him. 1 Peter 2:9 says, "*But you are a chosen race, a royal priesthood, a holy nation, a people for His own possession, that you may proclaim the excellencies of Him who called you out of darkness into His marvelous light.*"

When people use the word salvation without including Jesus Christ's work on the cross, they are likely referring to their own heightened state of awareness about themselves. Salvation in Christ is offered for the freedom of your soul for today and into eternity. You move from darkness into His marvelous light! Salvation in yourself keeps you bound to your human limits and reliant on constant reflection of your life and actions. It's a lifetime of hard labor and chasing after a "higher self." I'm not sure that even my "higher self" would be able to manage that kind of work for the rest of my life. We have hope in God because of the work that has already been done on the cross (John 3:16), not because of the future work we hope He will do. As culture invites us into a lifetime of inner work, we can rest in the completed work over our tired, worn out, and exhausted lives. In God's grace and mercy, my soul finds real rest in the power and guidance of my Designer and Creator.

5 THE SELF JOURNEY

Can I be transparent? This chapter scares me the most. There is a lot of room for misinterpretation and misunderstanding. The goal of the book is to illuminate the cheap messaging that is drawing Christian women into a dead-end journey of self, to hold it against the Light of truth, and to fully follow Jesus. But in order to do that, we have to identify the very thing that is holding us back from freedom in Christ in order to get there. It will be uncomfortable because, at some point, all of us will identify with a stage. Whether we are currently in it or not, we will see ourselves somewhere on the path. If we find ourselves in a certain stage, we will also be able to see what stage we are headed for next. My prayer is that God will do a work in us, in me, and in you—a work that causes us to pause, reflect, repent where necessary and turn our hearts fully toward Christ.

In this chapter, we are going to walk through each stage of what I call the self-discovery journey, the fairytale, that is leading women, Christian and non-Christian women alike, to the destination of self as god. We've identified what that "cheap messaging" of a self-focused life looks like, we've talked about Alissa's, Candace's, and Asia's relationships to the self-love journey, and now we will walk the paths together. We are putting to bed the saying, "What you don't know won't kill you," because, when it comes to the journey of self, our lack of awareness can lead us out of alignment with Christ and directly to the dead-end of living for ourselves.

We are seeing more of the New Age beliefs filling spaces in our world that include healing through crystals, cards, and natural remedies like mushrooms. But, that does not represent the majority of women today. Not yet, at least. Most of us wouldn't step into something so obviously "different" such as those practices. But most of us are taking a journey that is just as destructive without even realizing it. It's called the "Self-Journey." And as with all journeys, there is a starting point, events along the way, and a final destination.

The journey is already mapped out. It may not yet be clear to you, but since the beginning of time, the journey has been plotted from start to finish in order to steal your heart, mind, and soul away from God. The Self-Journey map looks like this: **left unchecked, self-care can turn into self-discovery, self-love, self-acceptance, self-reliance, and then self as god.**

Self-Care

Before you close the book out of annoyance that self-care would be in the lineup here, please know that I'm a mom of two girls and I know what it's like to need a moment to myself. In the 2,000 or so square feet of our house, my girls and I typically share the same couch cushion, the same chair in my workspace, the same sink in my bathroom, and, well everywhere else. Being alone only happens when they are sleeping. Self-care can feel like a true luxury.

I would classify my fitness time self-care. I would call getting my fake lashes filled self-care. Resting when I have a migraine is self-care. Using sunless tanner on my very pale, Dutch skin is self-care (and it's just thoughtful for all of those people around me as well). Running through the Starbucks drive-thru multiple days a week is self-care (also potentially self-sabotage on my nervous system and bank account, but that doesn't stop me). Self-care is totally acceptable, and it's important to understand the things that can help you take a mental and physical break from the grinding daily routine. Self-care can also be important if you have an ailing issue physically or mentally. If you are not healthy or have a hard time functioning mentally in the day-to-day, then taking a step toward understanding the issue to get better does matter.

So why does self-care make up the first step of self-journey? Because it's the first point of dedicated care and focus on ourselves. We don't just practice it; we also preach it from the rooftops. We use self-care to sell products, solve each other's problems, and escape from the world. And it's here that we are championing each other straight to the mirror—right to the place where, if we aren't careful, we will begin a journey of going beyond a "mommy timeout" to a pattern of escaping in order to find greater levels of happiness and peace within ourselves.

Here's the truth about self-care: the very need for self-care arises from the same limitations that should make us dependent on God.

We are desperate for an outlet. The Google search definition of self-care is "the practice of taking an active role in protecting one's own well-being and happiness, in particular during periods of stress." Self-care is used as a reaction to and a temporary relief from stress. Many women also talk about self-care as a preventative for stress. Stress is just about as common as breathing at this point in history. In fact, WebMD.com says that 75-90% of all doctor's visits are for stress-related ailments and complaints. I'm sure that stresses doctors out too.

Can I point something out? Jesus felt stress. This matters because Jesus can care for us in our stress. You and I could sit for years and talk about what stress has done to our lives, but I think we often forget that Jesus knew stress too. Throughout His ministry, Jesus would sneak away from the overwhelming crowds. He didn't go find a calm place to chill out and unwind with a hand-crafted coffee drink. Jesus would get away to pray. Luke 5:15-16 says, *"Yet the news about him spread all the more so that crowds of people came to hear him and to be healed of their sicknesses. But Jesus often withdrew to lonely places and prayed."*

In St. Luke Vol. 1, "The Pulpit Commentary", H.D.M Spence, an Anglican author said, "Jesus Christ could not have poured out his heart to his Father as he did, and gained the refreshment and strength he gained in prayer if he had remained in the midst of the curious and exacting throngs who waited upon him. He withdrew Himself into the wilderness. We have an intimation that he had to make a very strenuous effort to escape from the multitudes and to secure the seclusion he desired. But He made it. And we shall be wise if we do the same." Spence notes, "If strength [Jesus] needed to pray, how much more weakness [us]!".[9]

In His moment of greatest stress, Jesus actually experienced hematidrosis which is a condition in which people can sweat blood when they are under extreme stress such as facing death. His final moments before being arrested and crucified were filled with stress and agony. Luke 22:44 says, "*And being in agony He prayed more earnestly; his sweat became like great drops of blood falling down to the ground.*"

I will not downplay stress. Nor will I pretend that stress has a quick and easy solution. No, the world we live in today demands so much of our brain space, physical energy, and emotional energy that stress is here to stay. Jesus didn't downplay stress either. He never said, "go and stress no more." But He did tell us to pray, and He taught us that by His own example. Jesus used stress as a trigger to get to the Father as soon as possible.

The self-journey starts here in the most unsuspecting place of self-care, because stress and life's overwhelming seasons require a remedy. We will either run to God or to ourselves, but there has to be a starting point, and I believe self-care is the launching pad. You may disagree with me, and that's ok. No one finds herself on a journey completely focused on herself overnight. No one finds herself miles off course or feeling a world away from God overnight. Self-care is the starting point that can set the self-journey into motion. That first initial glance inward is not the problem. But it's in self-care that we can find ourselves either inviting Jesus into the process of

9 H D M Spence-Jones, Joseph S Exell, and Edward Mark Deems. 1983. The Pulpit Commentary. Grand Rapids, Mich.: Eerdmans.

healing, recovery, rest and finding the peace we need or not. It's here where we choose that Jesus is either our Sustainer and greatest Companion or that He is not. Knowing that He knew the highest level of stress that a human can experience and yet God was the only thing on His mind helps us to remember that "self-care" is not the solution to our problems: God is. Communication through prayer is our lifeline. God's presence alone can heal us: Philippians 4:6-7 says, "...*do not be anxious about anything, but in everything by prayer and supplication with thanksgiving let your requests be made known to God. And the peace of God, which surpasses all understanding, will guard your hearts and your minds in Christ Jesus.*"

Self-Discovery

The next step on the journey becomes clear as we begin picking up speed on the path; self-discovery begins the more intentional "deep dive" into our inner part in order to determine who we are, why we do what we do, and what our real character looks like. We have people handing us the tools every day on social media and in our real lives to help "discover the real us." From everything like the Enneagram to Psychics, we are told that we need to understand ourselves in order to live our best lives. (Which is ironic, believing that a test, stars in the sky, or a stranger could know the true you, but I digress.)

Some questions we are invited to ask ourselves include the following:

- How do your thoughts shape the way that you see yourself or the world around you?
- How are the words you are speaking to yourself building or demolishing your self-esteem?
- Are you taking care of yourself or giving your life away to other people?
- Is the work you are doing now serving you best? Are the people in your life serving you?

The goal of discovering our true self is to gain confidence in the person of you: inner, social, physical, and psychological. Self-confidence comes with the promise that our lives will improve because we will feel good about ourselves no matter what anyone says or thinks. Self-confidence impacts the way that we interact with our world, and we all need enough of it to function amongst other human beings. But the level of self-confidence that I'm referring to is the pursuit of self-confidence that steals our availability to obey God's purpose on our lives. Our culture throws self-confidence around as the first-place prize. Find self-confidence at any cost! Don't get me wrong, I desperately want my daughters to be confident in their abilities and to understand their worth and beauty. For this reason, I don't talk about the way I feel about my body in front of them. I apologize when I mess up and I don't shy away from telling them when I'm scared or frustrated or when I simply don't know the answers to things.

Most importantly, I want them to know a lesson I've learned: the self-confidence I try to create on my own lasts only as long as I determine it. But the confidence in whom God has made me comes from Him. As my personal Designer and Creator, He has assigned that worth to me already. This is the best news: I can't escape the identity God assigned to me.

Self-discovery, and the self-confidence that it breeds, left unchecked and left in our own hands may lead us to the next stage of the journey: self-love.

Self-Love

HOLD ON, what could I possibly say about self-love that could challenge such a beautiful concept?

We often confuse self-love with self-worth. They are not the same thing. Without God, we have to find ways to love ourselves in order to feel worthy. But God, who invented Love because it's literally who He is, placed love and worth on us long before we would even understand the terms self-love or self-worth. More on this to come later in this section.

What about the importance of loving ourselves first? **Don't we need to love ourselves first in order to love others and to love God?** Some people have said, "You can't pour from an empty cup." In other words, you can't give to others what you don't have yourself. As I invited women into the discussion for this book, I asked a question; "What does self-love mean to you?" About 80% of women, Christian and non-believers, said that self-love was required before they could understand God's love or give love to other people.

Before I go on, let me plant this seed: with God, an empty cup of love doesn't exist. In fact, when you know God, you know love in its fullest and most unfiltered form, and you hold a full cup of it at all times.

But let's get back to dissecting the idea that you have to love yourself before you can contribute to the people in the world around you. This idea conceptually works. To hate ourselves is a roadblock to many things, including an unhindered partnership with God. To spend so much of our day loathing who we are or how we are naturally wired is to miss out on the joy of walking with Jesus. So, naturally, we would assume that you must love yourself and find a healthy mindset in order to be useful to anyone else. It's the oxygen-mask-on-an-airplane analogy: "put your own mask on before helping others." But, we've left out one big detail in these statements: Jesus and His power. We've shouldered the responsibility of solving the "love your neighbor as yourself" verse by assuming that we are responsible for our own filling and our own strength to accomplish it. But Jesus speaks into this:

> Hearing that Jesus had silenced the Sadducees, the Pharisees got together. One of them, an expert in the law, tested him with this question: "Teacher, which is the greatest commandment in the Law?" Jesus replied: "'Love the Lord your God with all your heart and with all your soul and with all your mind.' This is the first and greatest commandment. And the second is like it: 'Love your neighbor as yourself.' All the Law and the Prophets hang on these two commandments." (Matthew 22:34-40)

Notice the commandments Jesus gives: first, love God

with all of your heart, and second, love your neighbor as yourself. When Jesus says to love your neighbor as yourself, He is describing a concern for their welfare and wellbeing, not a love that approves of itself and walks in self-confidence. It is here that we create a false interpretation of this passage. Jesus meant love in action, meeting basic needs that we would meet for ourselves. The good Samaritan in Luke 10 shows us how to love our neighbor as he met the man's physical needs to the best of his ability. To love our neighbor means to be most concerned about meeting their basic physical needs just as we are most concerned about our own physical needs. At our core, we want to make sure that we don't starve, that we have a place to lay our heads and that our children are safe from harm. These are the welfare concerns that we have for ourselves, and Jesus is describing here. He says to love by meeting the needs of our neighbors, just like we meet our own needs.

John 13:34 says, *"A new commandment I give you: Love one another. As I have loved you, so you should love one another."*

Jesus didn't give a third command that we must love God, love ourselves, and then love others as a result of the first two commandments. Loving others is not a byproduct of the way that we feel about ourselves. Because people give in to temptation, we gossip, slander, throw each other under the bus, deceive, manipulate, and live in unhealthy codependent friendships and relationships. Jesus spoke the correct words in the correct order, leaving nothing out: Love God, and love your neighbor as yourself.

Self-Acceptance

Once we've learned to love ourselves, we take the next step of the journey toward self-acceptance.

In large, we've moved away from self-improvement because of the amount of work that it required. Most people felt like they would never be able to do enough to feel confident in who they were. They couldn't keep up. Self-acceptance limits us to what we know about ourselves and how we feel about ourselves. And, self-acceptance, at the end of the day, is still something to be achieved.

Candace, who ached for acceptance from others through perfectionism, was told that as she walked the road of her self-discovery journey and found self-acceptance, that a door would unlock the peace and contentment that she was looking for. What she found was a door that opened to another door, then another, then another. She was promised that she could finally rest from her striving to please people and forget about what they think. "No one's opinion matters but yours," people would say.

But didn't the Bible say somewhere that we are supposed to consider others better than ourselves? (Phil. 2:3-4) Candace felt pulled in two different directions. What she didn't realize as she followed the journey of the self is that self-acceptance, pursued apart from God, actually kept her blind to the things that she needed to surrender in her life—the biggest one being pride. Our culture's version of self-acceptance says that you are the most important variable in your life, and everything else must fit into your fortified space of happiness, or else it shouldn't get close. God and His truth usually fall into that category. Because God often protects us from ourselves in uncomfortable ways, we can push Him away in order to preserve our personal peace.

For example, the Holy Spirit may be causing us to pause right now as we are talking about self-acceptance. He may be asking us to change our pursuit from learning to love ourselves, to learn to love Him most. When we are tempted to make ourselves feel better in a discouraging moment with a mantra like, "I'm more than enough right now," we can instead pray, "God, because of Your love and power I am made permanently enough."

Self-acceptance can make one feel independent of the identity that God has placed on her. Accepting oneself just the way that she is will only make sense when one is tattooed with the identity of Jesus. We face an identity crisis any time we attempt to understand ourselves apart from what our Creator has said about us. It's like a piece of art trying to describe why it was painted the way that it was, and what its purpose is, without ever consulting the artist who created it. Like the painting, we can't know ourselves fully until we understand where we came from and why. Knowing our identity requires understanding our Maker.

Ephesians 1 says, "*For He chose us in Him before the creation of the world to be holy and blameless in His sight. In love, He predestined us for adoption to sonship through Jesus Christ, in accordance with His pleasure and will—to the praise of his glorious grace, which he has freely given us in the One He loves.*" Not only do we have the royal seal on our hearts, but we also have the hope of spending eternity with God. Nothing that we can say or do will take that away from us. Praise God!

Once we find acceptance, we are faced with the next stage of the journey. Are you fatigued yet? Wipe the sweat from your brow and let's keep going. This is important stuff. Our current step of worldly self-acceptance may lead us next to self-reliance instead of reliance on God and His power.

Self-Reliance

Once we've reached the place where we no longer consult God about our lives, we have committed fully to the self-reliance path. The leg of this journey may just be the most deceitful of all. Why?

Because relying on ourselves is tangible and logical. We can see it, touch it, experience it, and we can make sense of doing things ourselves. We can get through most of our lives without consulting God for things like job changes, having children, going to school, revolutionizing our life with CrossFit (ok, you know I had to plug it).

To be honest, I've always struggled with this concept of supporting myself with my daily needs and habits versus being fully reliant on God. If you've ever been confused like me, I want to share with you what I've learned; God wants to be involved in ever part of it. Colston once taught our youth students how to involve God in every area of their life by drawing a circle and drawing lines to look like slices of pizza within the circle. In each slice, he wrote a different part of our lives: school, work, fun, relationships, God, church, etc. After he filled in the slices, he explained that we view life like a circle, where everything has its own compartment, including God. But the way that God wants us to live looks more like God being in every compartment. God should be in every slice of our lives.

This means that we rely on Him for everything, even the next breath that we take. He also gives us the chance to choose the next step of our lives based on the boundaries written in His Word. Those boundaries aren't restricting; they are what set us free. Boundaries of loving others so that we don't fall too far in love with ourselves. Boundaries to spend time with Him so that we can know the truth and live with it daily. Boundaries to make our life about sharing the Gospel so that our lives can bring glory to God in the next life. Boundaries that make it possible for God to say, "Well done, my good and faithful servant" when we reach heaven.

Relying on ourselves is an illusion that will keep us from living this life to the full because without Jesus, we can only tap into the limited human strength. I need His strength every day. Every single day.

Self as god

What started as misplaced self-care led to self-acceptance, then to self-love, then self-reliance, then inevitably, to self as god. The journey to get to self as god can be slow, but it's getting faster and faster in our current culture, mainly because of social media. Some women will dabble, and some will test the waters, while others dive head-first into the rip current out of desperation to find a source of peace.

I wish I was making this up. I wish that not a single human being would ever get to this point in their existence, but we are here because self as god is trendy. It's actually the OG sin as we discussed in chapter one, but Satan keeps bringing it back like bangs or mom jeans.

We've decided that God or a form of God can only exist if it validates us and our existence. Does this relationship make me better? Does this job bring me happiness? Does my environment bring me only peace? Does this church meet all of my preferences and desires?

I didn't write this book solely for those who are on the fence about God. I wrote this book because even committed followers of Jesus are finding themselves dabbling with the self-discovery journey that will inevitably bring them to this very grim dead end. Friends, if Adam and Eve, who knew God and walked in the only perfect place to ever exist on planet earth, could fall for the deception of self as god, then no one, I repeat no one is exempt. And the enemy is clever as all get out. He aims his arrows right where we are most susceptible: our needs to feel loved, beautiful, and full of purpose. He replaces the truth with the lie that pursuit of knowing ourselves will achieve these needs.

Remember, the self-journey is very hard to detect today. In fact, you may be reading this book and realize that you've reached this stage of the journey, unaware and a little bit shaken. We've got to live with our guard up. Someone who has reached self as god doesn't look threatening, and they don't look desperately lost from the outside. In fact, many people who have chosen to do life without the One True God, seem content to keep doing the work and celebrating their efforts. But what is the cost of this final destination?

"Not everyone who says to me, 'Lord, Lord,' will enter the kingdom of heaven, but only the one who does the will of my Father who is in heaven. Many will say to me on that day, 'Lord, Lord, did we not prophesy in your name and in your name drive out demons and in your name perform many miracles?' Then I will tell them plainly, 'I never knew you. Away from me, you evildoers!'" Matthew 7:21–23

[10] Peterson, Eugene H. 2017. The Message : The Bible in Contemporary Language. Colorado Springs: Navpress.

The Message paraphrase says it like this: *"Knowing the correct password—saying 'Master, Master,' for instance—isn't going to get you anywhere with me. What is required is serious obedience— doing what my Father wills. I can see it now—at the Final Judgement thousands strutting up to me and saying, 'Master, we preached the Message, we bashed the demons, our God-sponsored projects had everyone talking.' And do you know what I am going to say? 'You missed the boat. All you did was use me to make yourselves important. You don't impress me one bit. You're out of here.'"*[10]

The irony of the self as god destination is that eternity is only accessible through denial of self in order to accept the salvation that is offered through Jesus Christ. We are unable to contribute a single thing to our salvation.

But get this: *"For just as through the disobedience of the one man [Adam and Eve] the many were made sinners [humanity], so also through the obedience of the one man [Jesus Christ] the many will be made righteous."* Romans 5:19.

Even here, hope is not lost. (Read that again.) No matter how far we take the pursuit of our "highest self," we are still redeemable when we choose to put Jesus back on the throne that we've been sitting on. But we have to make a move. We have to raise the cry of our life up to Jesus and repent (turn away completely) from our pursuit of self.

Journey to ONE Destination; We Can't Serve Two Masters

No, you can't keep yourself and pursue Jesus at the same time. Jesus said, *"No one can serve two masters. Either you will hate the one and love the other, or you will be devoted to the one and despise the other. You cannot serve both God and money."* Matthew 6:24

You can't have a lot of Jesus and a small pursuit of self on the side. You can't have equal parts Jesus and arrogant self-love. You can't serve two Masters of God and self. Only one gets the throne.

You can't figure yourself out without Jesus. As we've discussed, it's impossible to know yourself fully apart from your

Creator. We have to stop trying to balance both by talking about Jesus and also about self-discovery. The beautiful thing about choosing Jesus is that you will lose the desire to pursue yourself. When you know Him, you know yourself-- the ugly side of your past, full of sin, and the redeemed side of today and eternity, stamped with Jesus' love and approval. You will see yourself through His eyes, and you will feel your heart begin to beat to the rhythm of a new person—fully alive to life and filled with purpose that will extend far beyond yourself, right into eternity.

There is a narrow path that extends off of the self-as-god destination. The narrow path leads to real hope and redemption through Jesus when we understand the full weight of His life-giving offer through repentance. Not many people will turn from themselves at this point in the game, which is why that road is narrow. But my greatest prayer for you and for me is that our eyes would be opened here and that we would know this narrow path, to feel its terrain under our feet and feel the warmth of its light and hope on our faces. Let's make our choices to walk toward Jesus and never look back.

Where Do You Stand on the Path?

Knowing the self-discovery journey stages opens the doors for understanding. To review, the journey begins with self-care and moves to self-discovery, self-acceptance, self-love, then to self as god. We can now ask ourselves, what stage of the journey can I currently identify with most? What lies did I accept from the previous stage that brought me to the next one?

You may be in the self as god phase if:
- You have found yourself only attracted to hearing about a loving God while dismissing the more "difficult" aspects of God's nature, such as the demand to die to self.
- You have dismissed God or the church due to their inability to serve you or make you comfortable in your faith.
- Nature and blessings cause you to turn inward and not toward God.

- Your life's plan doesn't include following Jesus and saying yes to God's plan.

God knew about the self-discovery journey from the beginning of time. Blessed are we that He sent Jesus to make a new way, to crucify the old, and renew our strength in His Name. Don't take another step without Him.

6 THE
IDENTITY CRISIS

We aren't broken because we let our self-care routine turn into full-blown self-obsession. We operate as broken people because of something even deeper: an identity crisis.

I felt the merciless weight of my own identity crisis at 19 and based on the amount of time we are spending trying to become the best versions of ourselves, many of us are battling our own identity crisis right now. Who would we be if we lost our successful careers? Who would we be if we didn't have children to take care of? Who would we be if our social media followings disappeared? Who would we be if our physical appearance was dramatically altered in some way?

To find our way off of the wide path and onto the narrow path to find our identity from the right Source, we have to know this: The reason that we embark on the journey of self comes from an identity crisis. Read that sentence again if you must, then let's get to work.

An Identity Issue

The journey of self that we discussed in the last chapter is one for which we have to work; we must work to gain knowledge, work to become our better selves, work to let go of the past, then continue working to keep our momentum. When we work hard for something, we tend to attach our identity to it.

There are three places in which I'm constantly trying to find my worth and identity: the world, myself, or God. Only one can win. They can all impact us, but we will be shaped and molded by one of the three. For years I sought desperately to find my worth and identity in my reputation of being a model which was handed to me at 15 years old. I, quite literally, lived each day hoping that I would be accepted by strangers in passing at Target, or at the pool, or at social gatherings. I've sought desperately to find my identity and worth in myself as I've worked hard to be known for something important, be it a job or accomplishment. But, by far, the ultimate peace has come when I've looked beyond myself and beyond the world around me to find my significance in God alone.

The search for our identity can lead to physical ailments. Yes, our pursuit of identity can make us sick. Physical ailments tend to tie back to the spiritual issues of brokenness, pride, and selfishness. I've always had "stress stomach aches" as I call them. Some call them "nervous bellies" or "anxious tummies." I was diagnosed with IBS in college. The doctor kept telling me that I was stressed, which I already knew, but could stress really cause so many stomach issues and weight issues? Yes, yes it could. Harvard Health recently published an article called, "The Gut-Brain Connection" that explains how stress impacts the gut and how the gut impacts stress.

If you drop a pin on the timeline of my life, I will tell you that I was dealing with one of these issues in some way, shape, or form. My anxiety, gut issues, and panic attacks came at the hands of my broken human nature that wanted to control every detail. I didn't trust that I was fully enough because of God Who lived in me. My body image issues were rooted in my choice to believe that what the world said about my body mattered more than what God had already said. My daily battle with stress came from the need to control everything to go as I planned it to go. Physical ailments don't equal punishment. That is not how God operates. You are not a puppet that He punishes when the strings get all tangled up. He lovingly works through the untangling, which can often be a long and tedious project full of doubt, and waiting, and living tangled.

From the beginning, we have to make a decision of where we are going to begin searching for healing and restoration. Knowing that any physical ailment that we have are ultimately linked to a spiritual issue will position our hearts and minds to see our struggles in the right light.

Also, knowing that an identity crisis—not knowing where to find our worth and purpose—is likely to blame for our searching gives us the ability to start the healing process in a productive place: at the feet of Jesus. When He said, "*come to Me, all of you who are weary and burdened, for I will give you rest*" (Matt. 11:28) Jesus wasn't making some sort of spiritual ploy for the weak. The world will tell you that seeking God's healing is a cop-out and an escape from doing the work it takes to get better. But, when we understand that the work of achieving wholeness and salvation has already been finished by Jesus' death on the cross, we won't have to spend our lives working for what's already been accomplished for us. God eliminated the work! (Let that sink in) God has eliminated the striving, the "rising above," the need to find "power from within," all because He loves us so much and because He possessed the power we lacked to do so. 1 Peter 2:24 clearly shows us, "'*He Himself bore our sins' in his body on the tree, that we might die to sin and live to righteousness. 'By His wounds you have been healed.'*"

An unloving Father would leave us to figure it all out on our own, but not God. We have to understand the basics of self-care through the messages of the "Good News" of the Gospel. And what is basic self-care in the Bible? It is losing our lives for Jesus' sake in order to find life. You can see this truth in Matthew 10:39, "*Whoever finds their life will lose it, and whoever loses their life for my sake will find it.*" Without God, we will continue an effort of search and rescue for ourselves that will come up empty-handed every time.

God has the ability to set us free from the devastation of sin's curse. He invites us in for the sake of our spiritual well-being, then for our physical well-being. God fights for the healing of our hearts more than He will fight for our physical healing.

Five years ago I heard a pastor say something profound right before he walked us through the entire Bible from start to finish, which he accomplished in 45 minutes: "God has been at work to fix us and our sin problem ever since the beginning." I've not been able to shake that statement as it now changes how I see everything. This is the foundation of the Gospel that turns our lives 180 degrees in the other direction. God is fighting to fix our hearts above all else. We tend to want to settle for the Band-Aid of self-care while He is inviting us into wholeness in Jesus' Name.

Even in the moment of chaos when your children are screaming and you're done parenting for the day. Even in the moment where you've beat yourself up for not eating healthy enough. Even when you can't get the dark cloud of emotions and negative thoughts to lift. Even when you are physically impacted by your anxiety. Yes, especially in these moments, God is fighting to fix the brokenness. While the world cheers you on to dive deeper within yourself—encouraging you in your feeble state that you're somehow strong enough to rise above it —God is aware and working on your behalf.

God hasn't created a 2000 piece puzzle out of your identity. He isn't testing you. He's inviting you to receive and put on the identity that He is offering to you. This identity is one that was created specifically for you, and when you live in this identity, you live fully alive and fully free.

Identity Crisis Meets Jesus

My friend Asia knows a thing or two about an identity crisis. She was just 11 months old when her mom and dad, Detroit, Michigan residents, walked out of the hospital holding their new adopted little girl. Asia was born with a severe cleft palate, unwanted by her birth mom. After her first of many surgeries, she was released to her new parents as they started their life together as a family of three.

Growing up, Asia was well aware of her adopted status although she never felt adopted until she looked in the mirror.

Her parents were Hispanic, and she was black. Asia was also well aware that her cleft palate left her face disfigured enough for people to notice, even after multiple surgeries and years of recovery. The scars remained. Asia felt the sting of rejection on a daily basis as people stared, as little kids gawked, and as she would speak as clearly and confidently as she could through a mouth shaped differently than most. The rejection was so deeply rooted in her birth mom's abandonment that Asia, at a young age, became infatuated with this man called Jesus she kept hearing about from her parents. She learned about Him in Sunday school and was overwhelmed at the thought that her Creator could also be her Father and Protector and—best of all—that He could love His creation, a young girl with a disfigured mouth and adopted parents.

As a teenager Asia loved Scripture and how it taught her about the love God had for her, verses like Isaiah 54:10: *"'Though the mountains be shaken and the hills be removed, yet my unfailing love for you will not be shaken nor my covenant of peace be removed,' says the Lord, who has compassion on you."*

She held on tight to the identity she had as God's child, and not a child who was rejected by her birth mom. Asia clung to these words in 1 John 3:1, *"See what kind of love the Father has given to us in that we should be called God's children, and that is what we are! Because the world didn't recognize him, it doesn't recognize us."*

As an adult, Asia looks across the table at the women in her Bible study group at church and sees the identity crisis plaguing their lives. These women have experienced rejection from men, difficult children, infertility, bosses who don't see their value, traumatic childhoods, poor health, body image issues, abandonment by friends, and so much more. Every woman has a story. Every woman faces an identity crisis, just like Asia and just like you and me. Will the work we put into ourselves define us? Or will the complete work of love through Jesus define us?

The world tells us that an identity crisis gives us the freedom to become anything we want to be. The world encourages us women to fix our brokenness while ignoring the fact that we are all operating from a place of brokenness. A doctor in the emergency room would never ask a patient who has just come in with a severely broken back to figure out how they are going to work on themselves and find healing. No, the doctor who knows how to fix a broken back will be the best option for recovery and healing. We cannot meet our identity crisis with our inexperienced hands or those of other broken people.

Let me say it this way: We have full access to the Healer. Identity crisis, meet Jesus, The Perfect Son of God who died on two wood beams at 33 years old in order to pay the penalty of sin that humanity was incapable of covering. Jesus took our old identity of being hopeless and lost and gave us a new option: redeemed and forgiven. When we choose Jesus, our identity changes from lost to found. We move from an operating room table to a run in the park. We move from being rejected by people to a seat at God's table. Our identity crisis becomes identity confidence because of Jesus.

Self + Jesus

As we unravel our old identity and choose Jesus, we have to also look at the tangible areas of our lives. What does day-to-day life look like for one whose identity's roots are firmly planted in heavenly soil?

Caretaking is built into our nature. Survival is built into our DNA. We are hardwired to have to think about our hunger, our protection, our physical condition. As we meet our own needs, it can become less obvious that God is the one who is providing the food, the physical strength, and the opportunity for us to survive. The American culture of wealth and prosperity accelerates our need for more of more. We want happiness and wealth, safety and success, stuff and prestige. We want self and Jesus.

There was a rich man in the New Testament who encountered Jesus with a question. How could he have both self and Jesus? This guy was wealthy, but he wasn't whole. In the book of Matthew, in chapter 19, this man finds Jesus and asks,

"Teacher, what must I do to inherit eternal life?" He had everything life could offer, but eternity was out of reach. Jesus put to bed the idea that any person could live for himself and for Jesus at the same time: *"If you want to be perfect, go, sell your possessions and give to the poor, and you will have treasure in heaven. Then come, follow me."* The ultimatum was given; wealth or Jesus, not both.

It's not that Jesus doesn't want us to experience wealth, Jesus just knows our heart and how we crave all of the illusions that wealth seems to satisfy. Jesus wants us to need Him more than we need control over our life.

The rich man walked away sad because he had great wealth and he refused to give it up (verse 22). Choosing self left him only with a lifetime of wealth, and (because it's not written that he ever came back to Christ later in life) most likely an eternity of poverty and darkness, separated from God.

What's really happening when we believe that we can live for both God and ourselves? An identity crisis not yet resolved.

Jesus Minus Self

God eliminated the work, the striving, the "rising above," the "power from within" because He loves us so much. An unloving Father would desert us to figure things out for ourselves, but not God. He didn't just create the world and send Jesus to save it. Through man, He authored the Bible, our handbook for real life, so that we could know Him, hear from Him, and understand what He values.

We have to understand even the basics of self-care through the messages of the "Good News" of Jesus, the great news of the Gospel. Otherwise, we will continue an effort of search and rescue for ourselves that will come up empty every time. John 3:30 shows us the goal: *"'He must increase, but I must decrease.'"*

God isn't anti-self; God is anti-independence from Himself. Not because He is a control freak or a dominating force that we have to submit to out of fear—although many people view Him that way. When sin entered the world through Adam and Eve in the Garden, we lost our independence, or worse, we gained independence, and it proved our ruin. From the garden came an innate need for dependence because we were no longer in perfect harmony with God. There was a gap now that sin was created: God on one side, us on the other. We lost our wholeness, which is why we have to choose who we will depend on, ourselves or God.

To fix our lack of wholeness, God sent Jesus. Jesus was the Perfect Sacrifice, a human who did not sin and lacked nothing, in order to make right what was so wrong with humanity. Jesus did what we are incapable of doing for ourselves; He paid our sin penalty in full. Isaiah 53:5 says, "*But He [Jesus] was wounded for our transgressions [intentional sins]; He was crushed for our iniquities [premeditated sin and unrepentance]; upon Him was the chastisement that brought us peace, and with His stripes, we are healed.*"

When it comes to spiritual wholeness, the competition of self vs. Jesus isn't even close. Jesus died for you so that you don't have to live for yourself. He died for you so that you don't have to spend a lifetime working on a better you. He made that instantaneously possible for you on the cross. God invites our souls to rest. We can't rest if we are trying to find our worth and identity. The self-journey is not a restful journey, which is why God invites us to die to ourselves in order that He can do the work and fill us with our true identity.

One of my favorite leaders of women, the author and founder of IF: Gathering, Jennie Allen, says this, "The identities we're chasing will fail us again and again, but the identity that God gives if we'll grasp it, is substantial and changes everything. As long as I'm looking into myself for my identity, I'll either be self-righteous about how great I am, which is inaccurate, or distraught by the reality of the wreck I actually am." [11]

Like a lazy river that pulls you along at a steady, relaxing, and easy-going pace, such is the life of a woman fully dependent

[11] Jennie Allen. "Your True Identity." Lifeway. Accessed July 17, 2021. https://www.lifeway.com/en/articles/homelife-your-true-identity.

on God and the identity that He has wrapped around her. God's current of grace and love keeps us fully satisfied in Him, no longer needing to paddle ourselves and forge our own current. We are able to relax on our raft as it moves, humbled by God's goodness to stay there and float to wherever it is that He needs us to go.

7 THE
IDENTITY RESOLUTION

Awed by Magnificence but Enslaved to the Tangible

The Copeland family loves road trips. We make the 17-hour drive to Texas twice a year intentionally. I say "intentionally" because something funny happens to people's faces when we tell them how much we love to drive across the country as a family. My husband is a road warrior. He drives us through the night, chewing on sunflower seeds, listening to podcasts, and drinking coffee to stay awake. Every trip is an over-caffeinated adventure and a time for us to talk about our lives and dream about big what God may do next.

On one of our most recent trips to Austin, TX, we drove through patches of heavy rain. It felt like one monsoon after another as we drove in and out of walls of rain. After one particular downpour, we saw a double rainbow start to illuminate the sky. But, this wasn't just any rainbow: this rainbow grew and jumped out of the sky to showcase the most vibrant colors I have ever seen. It was as if God took highlighters out just for fun. Not only that, but this double rainbow touched the ground right next to our car. Had we not been driving 80 MPH, I'm convinced that we could have reached out and experienced what that color felt like.

We sat in awe, attempting to take pictures to capture it, but no phone could do this promise from God justice. But, let's be real; as awesome as this rainbow was, our attention was quickly diverted back to our devices. We returned to our screens to dump dopamine in our brains. God is amazing, but let's get back to our regular programming. Awe and wonder do fade... And it's no wonder that dopamine wins: pleasing ourselves with social media, a day of self-care, a healthy smoothie, or self-affirming quotes on our bathroom mirror keeps our brains and bodies happy.

If you haven't been personally in awe of Jesus the way that we were in awe of that double rainbow, then perhaps you're waiting on Jesus and not seeing Him in between the rain. Most women hold the belief that Jesus is an experience. We are taught from an early age that Jesus is a prayer away. We sing worship songs that invite the Holy Spirit into the room in order to experience Him. We are told that encounters with Jesus will change us, but we encounter ourselves far more often than Jesus.

It is no wonder that in the face of a decision to choose Jesus or self, self tends to win. Jesus feels like an experience to be had. Self is the person we live with and the one through whom we feel every emotion, ache, and longing. The tangible self will almost always take priority over the experience of Jesus. Jesus becomes an option because, like Alissa finding physical healing through a healthy diet, or Candace speaking daily affirmations over herself, daily maintenance of self tends to fill the gaps better than the pursuit of God-encounters. We are awed by the idea and magnificence of Jesus, but we are ultimately slaves to the tangible caretaking of ourselves.

Being slaves to the tangible is our choice as we ignore the magnificence of God. To break free, we have to admit that we have a sinful "old self" and drop her fast. She's holding us back and keeping us in a fruitless, shallow cycle.

I was desperate to love myself and my body for many years. I didn't realize that the ache I felt to love myself, could only be fulfilled if I put on a new self through Jesus, not a new body. The pursuit of loving myself would only keep me tied down to the old me, not a new and free me. Paul says in Ephesians 4:22-24, "*You were taught, with regard to your former way of life, to put off your old self, which is being corrupted by its deceitful desires; to be made new in the attitude of your minds, and to put on the new self, created to be like God in true righteousness and holiness."*

Our "old self" is the person we were before we've given our heart to Jesus. The old self, as explained by Paul as having "corruption by its deceitful desires" is incapable of righteousness because it doesn't yet have the holiness of God, which comes at salvation. The old self is disconnected from the Source of life. So Paul reminds the Ephesians that they had to put off their old self. As if it was a coat that was covered in bees, throw it off! Put on a new coat, a new self that is created to be like God in true righteousness. The promise of being like God that Eve was given in the Garden was a lie, but the guarantee to be given the righteousness and holiness of God at the surrender of salvation is a promise that God will fulfill. But we need a new self. Not a new outlook or perspective. Not enlightenment. Not a new form of consciousness. Not a new power within.

Identity Resolution

In Jesus, our identity is complete. While the world searches for an identity that it must create from experiences and desires, Jesus places on us His identity in a way that was designed purposely and individually for us before we ever existed. The identity crisis at the core of every woman is resolved through the new identity Christ won for us. Here's what knowing who you are looks like:

"And if the Spirit of Him who raised Jesus from the dead is living in you, He who raised Christ from the dead will also give life to your mortal bodies because of His Spirit who lives in you." – Romans 8:11

"I have been crucified with Christ and I no longer live, but Christ lives in me. The life I now live in the body, I live by faith in the Son of God, who loved me and gave Himself for me." – Galatians 2:20

"So you are no longer a slave, but God's child; and since you are His child, God has made you also an heir."– Galatians 4:7

Yet, while Scripture paints a portrait of truth, there still one thing keeping us from fully following Jesus into our identity resolution: our feelings.

Feelings vs. Facts

There is a difference between feeling love for ourselves emotionally and loving ourselves because of what we know to be true about ourselves. When I felt most unworthy of love, God used my then future husband to show me what it looked like to really beloved for the facts and not the feelings.

Colston and I began dating right in the middle of my freshman year of college-- when I hated how I looked most. My girlfriend and I planned a trip to go meet him for a weekend, as we were at Liberty University and he was attending Bible College in Missouri. I agonized over what to wear. Luckily for me, in 2007 the style amongst the Christian School crowd was flowy dress-like shirts with large, chunky jewelry to distract and draw the eye away from any unfavorable body parts. So, layers of flowy tops and gaudy costume jewelry it was.

There is a picture of us together from that trip to Nashville where he is smiling confidently in his short-sleeved polo and I'm wearing an oversized sweatshirt. I had the sleeves of my sweatshirt rolled up because I was undoubtedly sweating to death. It was a warm southern springtime day, but I was committed to that hoodie, and that hoodie was now stuck to me.

My husband speaks so casually about that time, even today, saying that he loved how I looked then just as much as he does now. I love him for it. I'm grateful that he loved me when I couldn't find it in me to love myself. This was the picture God needed me to see: a love that could see a much bigger picture than my limited and jaded view of myself. I'm aware of the good, the bad, and the ugly parts of me, but I can be loved in spite of those things. When I feel disappointed and ashamed of myself, there is one fact about me that makes me loveable; I was created and put together in God's image.

The world would say that I'm loveable because I'm worthy of love. But, being worthy of love simply for existing is much more complicated than it sounds. Being worthy (the definition being, "deserving effort, attention, or respect") of love isn't a given because of our person-ness. We didn't put our own cells together in the womb. We were given life as a gift—God literally gifted us with existence. But our worthiness doesn't come from simply existing. Rather it comes in the understanding that our lives were created for the purpose of glorifying God. There is only One who set our lives into existence and who instilled our purpose for living. The same One Who taught us the word purpose. The One who keeps our purpose moving in forwarding motion.

So if our Creator gave us existence and our existence gives us purpose, then that means that our worthiness comes from the same place: Creator God. To recap: I'm not loved because of what I can offer to people or to God. I'm not loved because of something that I've earned or learned. I'm not loved because I declare myself lovable. I'm not loved because I feel like I'm worthy of love, and I'm not loved because I should be loved.

The fact is that I am loved because God created me in His image. Don't let this familiar phrase remain stale or uninteresting. You and I were made after God Himself. It was out of His image that He produced our bodies, souls, and brains.

Genesis 1:26-27 says, "*Then God said, 'Let us make man in our image, after our likeness. And let them have dominion over the fish of the sea and over the birds of the heavens and over the livestock and over all the earth and over every creeping thing that creeps on the earth.' So God created man in his own image, in the image of God he created him; male and female he created them*" (emphasis added).

When we understand that we are not free agents, determining our own love and worth, then we begin cracking open the mystery of how we are supposed to love ourselves apart from feeling love for ourselves. We begin seeing the facts about who we are because we are created beings made in the image of the Creator, deemed worthy of His love because we are His creation. The facts are clear; we are loved enough to exist, we are worthy of love because of whom we are designed after, and we are able to love ourselves because we were loved first by God.

The Call

Out of that new identity comes the call to action. This call invites us to pick up our cross, die to self, and represent Christ to a world that doesn't know him:

Therefore, if anyone is in Christ, the new creation has come: The old has gone, the new is here! All this is from God, who reconciled us to himself through Christ and gave us the ministry of reconciliation: that God was reconciling the world to himself in Christ, not counting people's sins against them. And he has committed to us the message of reconciliation. We are therefore Christ's ambassadors, as though God were making his appeal through us. We implore you on Christ's behalf: Be reconciled to God. God made him who had no sin to be sin for us, so that in him we might become the righteousness of God. – 2 Corinthians 5:17-21

Not only is our identity resolved, but our life gains meaning far more important than happiness or success. Once we understand that the call requires us to take action, we can then have a deeper conversation about love. The call requires us to pursue self-giving vs. self-centered love.

Self-Centered Love vs. Self-Giving Love

Is it enough to simply know that we are loved by God in order to answer "yes" to His call and to live a life that is free from self-loathing, self-hate, etc.? Many women, those who follow Jesus and those who do not, would agree that they are created by God and loved by Him. But, based on the necessity of this book and the culture that we live in, that just hasn't seemed to take root deep enough for us. We are still believing that we have to find self-love and worth within ourselves. We are still desperately seeking validation around us. So, why is this? Why can't the love of God be enough?

Knowing that we are loved is one thing, but understanding what to do with that love is another. The world tells us to fill the voids of our life with love for ourselves. We are told that love covers all. But when we are invited to form a belief and understanding about love in our own life, we have to also form a belief about what that love calls us to do. Where the world would drive you right back to yourself to figure it out, God showed us a picture of what we are to do with that love: "*For our sake he made him to be sin who knew no sin, so that in him we might become the righteousness of God.*" – 2 Cor. 5:21

The love that God designed is one that first gives before it would consider taking. Jesus was the ultimate representation of self-giving love. He didn't get it wrong. He didn't set the bar too high for us. God is not asking that you become a monk. He's asking that you take the love that you have been given and use it for the good of that purpose you were born with.

The world tells you to take this love, first make sure you have a healthy dose of it for yourself, and then go out and help other people. But God didn't require that of Jesus, and He is not requiring that of you either. He's inviting us to love Him first and out of that love that calls us worthy because of Him, to then go and love other people.

Pay attention to the marketing and advertising all around you that encourages self-centered love. While it is said perhaps with good intentions, it is most often spoken with a lack of knowledge about where real love came from, therefore, we have to reconsider it. Hear my heart when I say this: If you are unsure of what love is supposed to be, don't listen to other people who are also trying to figure it out. Find your way to the Source. Immerse yourself in Scripture that explains Who Love is and how that totally and radically changes you. God's love didn't just get me through a tough season of body image darkness, His love gave me new eyes to see who I am and my purpose that far exceeds a feeling of love toward myself. Understanding love starts with Him, not with us.

Do we need to love ourselves first in order to love others and to love God?

But what about the importance of loving ourselves first?

In my research and in talking to women, the idea that we have to first love and care for ourselves in order to have anything to give to others was brought up a lot.

This idea conceptually works. To hate ourselves is a roadblock to many things, including an unhindered partnership with God. To spend so much of our day loathing who we are or how we are naturally wired is to miss out on the joy of walking with Jesus. So, naturally, we would assume that you must love yourself and find a healthy mindset in order to be useful to anyone else. It's the oxygen mask on an airplane analogy: "put your own mask on before yourself" or "Fill up your own pitcher before you have anything to pour into someone else." But, we've left out one big detail in these statements. Jesus and His power. We've shouldered the responsibility of solving the "love your neighbor as yourself" verse by assuming that we are responsible for our own filling and our own strength to accomplish it.

Jesus had this to say: *"Hearing that Jesus had silenced the Sadducees, the Pharisees got together. One of them, an expert in the law, tested him with this question: 'Teacher, which is the greatest commandment in the Law?' Jesus replied: ''Love the Lord your God with all your heart and with all your soul and with all your mind." This is the first and greatest commandment. And the second is like it: "Love your neighbor as yourself." All the Law and the Prophets hang on these two commandments.''* (Matthew 22:34-40)

The commandments that Jesus gives are to first love God with all of your heart and second, to love your neighbor as yourself. When Jesus says to love your neighbor as yourself He describes concern for their welfare and well-being. This is the main area where we create a false interpretation of this passage. Loving our neighbors doesn't require having positive feelings about who they are and how they live. To love our neighbor means to be concerned about their physical needs being met just like we are naturally most concerned about our own physical needs being met. At our core, it is revealed in difficult circumstances. We want to make sure that we don't starve, that we have a place to lay our heads, and that our children are safe from harm. These are the welfare concerns that we have for ourselves that Jesus is describing here. Loving your neighbor as yourself is a concern for the interest of others. Jesus says to love by meeting the needs of our neighbors, just like we meet our own needs.

John 13:34 says, "*A new commandment I give you: Love one another. As I have loved you, so you should love one another.*" The most important thing to note here is that Jesus didn't give a third command that we must love God, love ourselves, and then love others as a result of the first two commandments. Loving others is not a byproduct of the way we feel about ourselves, although most people live this way. It is why we gossip, slander, throw each other under the bus, deceive, manipulate, and live in unhealthy codependent friendships and relationships. When we fail to love ourselves fully in our own strength, then the people around us suffer as well.

Jesus spoke the correct words in the correct order, leaving nothing out: Love God, and love your neighbor as yourself.

Set Free from Self

Love sets us free. Every person on planet earth would agree that when we choose love, we become free from hate, free from anger, free from any kind of inner darkness. Love overrides it all, like the scene in the Wizard of Oz, when the world went from black and white to vivid color. The world defines love as a cure and as the answer to every problem in life. The world isn't wrong about love because it is the cure and it is the answer, but the world plus love without Jesus is only a fantasy of love, not the reality of it.

The reality of love is Jesus.

Jesus died so you could do more than learn to love yourself fully. Jesus died for your earthly and eternal freedom from your old self. When Jesus died on the cross, He over-rode our sin that was restricting us from having access to God. Our sin is a big, big deal. We can't love our way out of our sin. We can't decrease our sin by increasing our love. Sin is a barrier impossible for us to scale. So God sent Jesus to tear it down. The cross was the reach across the sin-crowded battlefield to win our hearts on the other side and to bring us safely home.

Martin Lloyd-Jones, an influential preacher and writer wrote a book about the cross titled (appropriately) *The Cross*, in which he emphasizes the sacrifice of Jesus in our place. In the last chapter of the book, he discusses the reality of how the cross sets us free from ourselves. While explaining the apostle Paul's conversion from a pious religious leader to a humbled servant of God, Martin quotes 2 Corinthians 5:17, "*If any man be in Christ he is a new creature: old things are passed away—behold all things have become new.*" Martin then says, "Nothing thrilled [Paul] more than the new view that he now had of himself. He had been liberated from all that old life [through the cross]. It was a terrible life when he really saw what it meant. It was a sham, it was a fraud; it was always insecure and it never gave real peace of heart, rest, and satisfaction. But now it is all different. The cross has really shown himself to himself." Martin continued, "Once a man sees himself in the light of the cross, he sees the horror of that self-centered view in its every aspect."[12]

The reality of love is that it calls us out, not inward or back toward self. The cross anchors us in the truth about this life; it's not about us, but about God. Real love sets us free to the bigger thing: to the betterment of other people, to the glory of God.

In Galatians 5:13-14, Paul says, "*For you were called to freedom, brothers. Only do not use your freedom as an opportunity for the flesh, but through love serve one another. For the whole law is fulfilled in one word: 'You shall love your neighbor as yourself.'*"

It's not a gift to find freedom; it's a command. It's not a journey of life to find freedom; it's a call to accept the responsibility. Paul tells us that our responsibility in this life is to use the love we've been given to give it back to the people in our world in Jesus' Name. God gives us every person and every relationship with "how to care for" instructions: *love them as yourself*

[12] David Martyn Lloyd-Jones, and Christopher Catherwood. 1986. The Cross : God's Way of Salvation. Westchester, Ill.: Crossway Books.

Love them as yourself before they love you back. This is a Jesus move. Real love loves before it understands. Real love loves before it decides how it feels about people.

So we flip the narrative; when the world instructs you to love yourself before you can love others, Jesus says to love others in order to unlock the deepest levels of love. You'll find love for yourself there because you will see God's love alive and tangible; you'll see God in you. And what do we do when we see God in ourselves? We level up. We leave ourselves behind without hesitation. We understand the cost of spending a lifetime loving ourselves rather than receiving God's love and giving love away. The joy is no longer found in feeling love for ourselves to enjoy this life. We choose to obey the command, to accept the responsibility of freedom, then we put on our dancing shoes. We throw off the constraints that we've placed on our own life that tie us down to the limited life lived for ourselves.

Then we dance.

Freedom pulls us out onto the dance floor, inviting us to let go of all fear, the desire to control, and the need to manipulate a journey of self-discovery that keeps us working and striving. We dance in the freedom from self as the beat of loving others pounds deeper into our chest, the rhythm of a life of service keeping us going, changing our perspective, and reshaping our love to look more like Jesus' love.

But you most certainly will not be dancing alone. God's way equals freedom from ourselves and freedom into a Divine partnership. He gives us the power of the Holy Spirit. This is important to note because our human nature draws us back to ourselves every moment that we are awake. We need all the help that we can get. Romans 8:11 says, *"And if the Spirit of him who raised Jesus from the dead is living in you, he who raised Christ from the dead will also give life to your mortal bodies because of his Spirit who lives in you."* A life that ripped Jesus out of His funeral clothes and out of the grave. Life that put breath back into His dead lungs. The same Spirit is in us, helping us live for the truth that God's glory, not our own, is life's highest priority.

As we learn to love God most and live daily in the reality of His love for us through Jesus, we experience the right side of the ultimatum: we live this life not on the path of the dead-end journey towards self, but on the path of freedom in God's love for us.

8 THE HERO

We've starved the fairytale by exposing its preexisting lies and sin-grown roots, and now we get to feast on the truth: there is one hero of our story and His name is Jesus. We can make good sidekicks, but Jesus will always be the better hero.

Oh, how I've prayed that this chapter will leave you breathless before God—in awe of Jesus, curious about His love for you and swept away in the joy that washes over His children when we hear His name. If you only knew what He did to save you. If you only knew His love without boundaries. If you only knew His constant presence. I want to make it absolutely clear: the real hero is Jesus. He always has been and always will be. There is nothing more reliable than this.

Being both God and man, He made the world and everything in it, including us, and everything *belongs* to him. Acts 4:12 tells us, *"And there is salvation in no one else, for there is no other name under heaven given among men by which we must be saved."*

Why is Jesus our Hero?

Better than the most untouchable celebrity, Jesus is famously for us. Jesus left the glory and spectacle of heaven, knowing that the depravity He would face on earth would be the agony of a broken creation, the heartbreak of human rejection, and a death in which He physically carried the sins of all of us. Mark 15:34 shows us the moment that He cried out to the Father on the cross, *"And at three in the afternoon Jesus cried out in a loud voice, "'Eloi, Eloi, lema sabachthani?'"* (which means "My God, my God, why have you forsaken me?")

Jesus was faithful to His Father and endured being alone without Him so that we don't have to. Evangelist Billy Graham says it this way, "As He died all our sins were placed on Him, and He became the final and complete sacrifice for our sins. And at that moment He was banished from the presence of God, for sin cannot exist in God's presence. His cry [in Mark 15:34] speaks of this truth; He endured the separation from God that you and I deserve."

While I make mistakes without considering the cost of the cross, Jesus knew every mistake I've ever made and went anyway. He obeyed the Father, and He stuck to the plan. While many Christians can be accused of using "scare tactics" in today's culture if they talk about hell, the reality of eternity exists: *"They [those who do not submit to Christ's Lordship] will be punished with everlasting destruction and shut out from the presence of the Lord and from the glory of his might."* 2 Thess. 1:9

But Jesus humbly stepped out of heaven to help us avoid an eternity separated from God. He fought for us at the expense of His own life. This is not normal, by the way. There is no other religion in which a god would sacrifice his own life for people, let alone people who hate him.

And while Jesus is our Hero and Rescuer, He is Satan's worst nightmare. The same enemy who is inviting us to lean on habits of self-care instead of Jesus is the same enemy who is rejoicing as we fully deny God with our self-obsessed lives. The enemy wins when we give him our curiosity about what the self-discovery journey could do for us. The enemy wins when we turn inward.

Might I add that Jesus is the worst thing that could have happened to Satan. Jesus is our lifeline to wholeness, the very thing that Satan has distorted and tried to deliver to us in cheapened ways. Satan wants to keep us on a hidden loop that circles back to our own deficiencies while dangling illusions of hope in front of us. Illusions such as significance through our achievements, approval through our appearance, and "meaningful" love that leans toward of loving ourselves more.

Jesus abolished the work that Satan uses as bait. He extends an invitation to rest while Satan extends a work order. And, if you've made it this far in the book, you know that a journey of self-discovery is a work order with a devastating consequence.

Jesus is the One our hearts are after, and when we enter into the beautiful exchange of dying to ourselves to take on the gift of His salvation, we enter into the most important identity resolution offered in this life through Jesus alone: newness.

This newness in our being is not something that God simply cleaned up, and it's certainly not a newness that we can re-create on our own. John 1:13 says of those who have placed faith in Christ, "*[they] were born, not of blood nor of the will of the flesh nor of the will of man, but of God.*" This newness we are given in Christ allows us to see the messaging of the world that says to love yourself most as the lesser option. Being a new creation in Christ means that old, dying, and dead things are now made new and holy, just like Paul said in Ephesians 4:24, "*and to put on the new self, created after the likeness of God in true righteousness and holiness.*"

Our Natural-Human Default Opposes God

As much as Jesus is the answer, without His redemption, our default is still toward sin and selfishness. While the world tells us that we are inherently good, the reality for humanity is that we are born bad and broken. Sin cripples us at the moment of conception and deteriorates our hearts, minds, and bodies as we grow.

Scripture says that we are born "children of wrath" in Ephesians 2:3: "*Among them we too all formerly lived in the lusts of our flesh, indulging the desires of the flesh and of the mind, and were by nature children of wrath, even as the rest.*" Scripture then says that from our very beginning we have "all sinned and fall short of the glory of God," in Romans 3:23.

Because of sin, our default state is to be in opposition or rebellion against God. It's not that we have the "wrong" formation; it's that our lifestyles and pursuits of the self are directly rebelling against God. Let's uncover this truth together so we can step into the light:

A self-seeking life opposes God: "But for those who are self-seeking and who reject the truth and follow evil, there will be wrath and anger. There will be trouble and distress for every human being who does evil: first for the Jew, then for the Gentile." Rom. 2:8–9

A self-seeking life leads to ruin: Romans 3:10–19 says, *"As it is written: 'There is no one righteous, not even one; there is no one who understands; there is no one who seeks God. All have turned away, they have together become worthless; there is no one who does good, not even one.' 'Their throats are open graves; their tongues practice deceit.' 'The poison of vipers is on their lips.' 'Their mouths are full of cursing and bitterness.' 'Their feet are swift to shed blood; ruin and misery mark their ways and the way of peace they do not know.' 'There is no fear of God before their eyes.' Now we know that whatever the law says, it says to those who are under the law so that every mouth may be silenced and the whole world held accountable to God."*

Milton Vincent, the author of *A Gospel Primer*, says, "Apart from Christ, I am also utterly deserving of and destined for eternal punishment in the Lake of Fire, completely unable to save myself or even to make one iota of a contribution to my own salvation."[13]

Our sin deserves death. Not just the death of life on earth, but the death of proximity to God. The payout for our sin should be that we are forever separated from God, His goodness, true light, and real Love. No takebacks, no do-overs. God's wrath against sin will be carried out in hell for all people who rebel against Him in life and death. There is simply no way to paint it in a better light, the consequences of our sin, even the smallest sin, is hell that never ends.

Just as unfair as eternal darkness and suffering seem for a little white lie, so is heaven and God forever for a helpless, sin-covered, and broken human being. Here is the gift most

---

[13] Vincent, Milton. 2008. A Gospel Primer : For Christians. Bemidji, Minn.: Focu Publishing.

undeserved: "*For the wages of sin is death, but the gift of God is eternal life through Jesus Christ our Lord*" (Romans 6:23).

Once we understand why Jesus is the better Hero of our story, we have to understand that there, in fact, can only be one Hero. Satan is trying to convince us that we can take Jesus' place, not in foreign countries with thrones and crowns, but in America with self-help and the pursuit of self-discovery.

So, despite God's gift of Jesus and salvation, we still find ourselves in a power struggle. We are rolling up our sleeves to first, get the power to fix ourselves. It doesn't always look this obvious though, right? Most people in our lives wouldn't even recognize our efforts to take control in order to fix ourselves. We wouldn't look at Candace's life and say that she is power-hungry. She was a victim of a selfish parent. She has lived her life like any other teenager and young adult, experimenting with the world around her. Candace was told that "no one else in this life would speak up for her" the way that she could speak for herself.

But, in her most tender and hidden places, the enemy planted seeds of illusion that she could take charge of her life and make it something new. As she put the effort in, she missed real newness in Christ and settled for a Band-Aid of positive thinking. The power struggle is not as obvious or dramatic as we would imagine on most occasions. The power struggle is anything that allows us to take control into our own hands in order to manipulate the life we think is best for ourselves. We may gain some ground and make our own dreams come true, but we will always be left to wonder what God could have done in and through us if He only had control.

God's Response to our Opposition

Any power struggle that we carry reveals our sin nature, the one that a Holy God should destroy altogether. Yes, our sin-filled heart deserves destruction. We shouldn't have a second chance, unlike the popular opinion that everyone is good and deserves a second chance. Our opposition to God is toxic and cannot mix with any true light from heaven. If He wanted to,

He could wipe us off of the face of the earth as quickly as He created it. We hardly take this as seriously as it is.

The miraculous act of love is not just that He has spared us from total destruction, but that He took action to save, renew, and redeem our hearts that stand against Him.

In His goodness, Christ died to atone for people who lived in opposition to God. Are you looking for a life-changing quote on your wall at home? One that stops people in their tracks and makes them think about their life? A sign reciting Romans 5:8 would be a good start: *"But God demonstrates his own love for us in this: While we were still sinners, Christ died for us."* Essentially, God is way better than us and proved it by saving us from eternal darkness when we didn't even like Him. Put it in a cursive font with a wood frame, and it would look great above the mantle.

The Struggle to Give the Power Back

We all fight for power over our lives, but when we choose to know Jesus, we experience the second kind of power struggle; giving the power back to God. Many of us are in the fight daily to give the power back to God. We push back against our flesh, what it wants, and what it can see and achieve. All the while we know that the best offerings of this life, in Christ, are the things that make an impact for the kingdom. The Kingdom is not just a destination of heaven, it is Jesus' spiritual empire that is accessible to all people who choose Him, and the Kingdom of Jesus is here now. In John 3:3, Jesus said, *"'Truly, truly, I say to you, unless one is born again he cannot see the kingdom of God.'"*

With all of my heart, I encourage you to keep fighting for Kingdom impact, not earthly self-discovery. Keep releasing the power back to God and allow Him to do the work as you begin to look less like yourself and more like Him.

Every move we make as Christ-followers will impact the spiritual kingdom (or not) and at the end of our lives, our satisfaction in His holiness and our surrender to His work in an through us (neither of which can be found in self) are the marks of a life well-lived. There are no signs of fairytale roots in a life well-lived for Christ.

Flourishing in the Desert

When Colston and I got married, we moved out to Southern California to work at a church there. After five years of comfort and CA bliss, we were let go from the church without warning. Hadley, our firstborn, was only three months old when we moved ourselves and our 150-pound French mastiff, Ruby, into an extended-stay hotel room until we could find another job.

As I shifted the basket of dirty laundry on my hip and pushed the baby stroller down the hotel halls, tears stung in my eyes and I could feel my face flush red. What was God doing? How could He take so much away from us all at once? To this day, the smell of a sterile hotel triggers memories of those moments, alone with God, unsure of where we would live next, or how I would emotionally recover.

God led us into the desert, figuratively and literally. Colston landed a job as a Discipleship Pastor and we moved to Odessa, Texas. I'll never forget flying over west Texas to interview for the church position. Looking out of the airplane window, I saw no trees, no water, and a lot of dust. I leaned over to Colston before we landed to say, "We can enjoy ourselves this weekend, but we cannot move here. To clarify, I will not live here." The joke was on me. Over the next two years, God radically changed my heart and life right there in the middle of the desert. I can still feel the sting of the shaggy bedroom carpet on my knees as I begged God to move us out of that desert.

God knew what He was doing. He removed friends, family, and any familiarity out of our lives so that He could get us alone. I hated it. Oh, how I hated it! But, in my anger and grasping for anything that would put my heart at ease, I began waking up early to sit with God. Like a child angry at a parent and fully dependent on them, I sat with Him. I cracked open my Bible and scribbled down notes from my frustrated perspective. And as time went on, He began to show me the rescue all over again.

God didn't answer my prayers for the physical things, people, and security that I begged Him for. God answered the needs of my heart and soul. He became everything that I thought I needed. He answered my prayer for a friend that was my closest confidant. He answered my prayer for security by proving that He would never leave me. Funny thing is that I seemed to feel His closeness most when I was expressing my anger toward Him. God answered my prayer for peace when everywhere that I looked around me was barren (literally, barren land and all).

More than realizing that Jesus wasn't just the answer for my eternal life anymore, I realized that Jesus had to guide every single step I took as Lord of my life. When I was stripped of everything that I knew during one meeting in California, God began a new work in me. He became like the air that I breathed. God wasn't just my Savior anymore, in order for me to get through the ups and downs of life, God had to become my Lord. In Hebrew, Lord means ruler or commander. I didn't often live by the loving commands of my Ruler, but by the feelings and desires of my own way.

In the desert, I couldn't move a muscle without Him because I was paralyzed by my circumstances. God rescued my soul when I gave my life to Him at four years old, but He was now rescuing my life, recalibrating my attention, and pulling me out of the riptide of figuring out how to live my life for me, in comfort and ease.

I learned the most important lesson of my life on the floor in the desert; Jesus is the prize. Nothing satisfies me like Him and nothing sinks deeper in my soul than the tangible presence of my Savior. He is close and He feels like peace and calm.

Jesus became the Hero of my every day (my struggles, identity, worth, popularity, etc.), not just the Hero of my death and eternity. This is what it's like to see God as Savior and Lord. Are you wishing that you could know God more intimately? Do you wish that you could experience Him as others do? You may have trusted God to redeem your heart, but are you trusting

God to redeem your days, hours, and minutes? Dying to self and starving the fairytale happen when we get out of the way and allow God to be God and Lord.

The Jesus that I met there in the desert was the One I had already given my life to, but I hadn't yet depended on Him. The moment that I depended on Jesus, and no longer on myself, was the moment I fell head over heels in love.

Jesus didn't just risk His life for us, He gave it in full. The Message Translation of Isaiah 53:12 says, *"Out of that terrible travail of soul, he'll see that it's worth it and be glad he did it. Through what he experienced, my righteous one, my servant, will make many 'righteous ones,' as he himself carries the burden of their sins. Therefore I'll reward him extravagantly— the best of everything, the highest honors— Because he looked death in the face and didn't flinch because he embraced the company of the lowest. He took on his own shoulders the sin of the many, he took up the cause of all the black sheep."*

The first thing that I know to be true about Jesus is this: I didn't get a mere glimpse of Jesus or a sample bite of His presence as I sat broken before Him. Milton Vincent, author of A Gospel Primer explains what I experienced: "Indeed, what makes the Gospel such great news is God, who brings me to Himself and then gives Himself so freely to me through Jesus Christ." I got full access to God through Jesus, access to His love, His forgiveness, and His company.

Why is this so important? Because Jesus stood in the gap between me and God. The fairytale doesn't hold that kind of power. Self and God are incompatible because of sin. Isaiah 59:2 says, *"But your iniquities have made a separation between you and your God, and your sins have hidden His face from you so that He does not hear."* A self-discovery journey doesn't accidentally or naturally end at God because there is a huge chasm between the two.

The second thing that I know to be true about Jesus is that He didn't rescue me to cover my life in bubble wrap. Jesus rescued me in order to wrap me in His mercy and grace to then to send me to go and do the most important work of making Him known to others.

Once I received rescue and followed Him as Lord, Jesus became the most precious relationship I've ever known. Nothing and no one compares to my Jesus. He's fighting moment-by-moment for my heart. He gives unmatchable gifts and loves me in my shame. He gets me, He knows my ugly, and He stays. He is too good for me to live for anything or anyone else. He is too faithful for me to chase other things. He is too loving for me to pursue a romance anywhere else. I can't compete with Jesus, and by His grace, I don't have to. He is the Hero of my story, and I pray that He is the Hero of yours, too.

My Hero, Jesus.

I was four years old when I first understood that Jesus was the hero of my story. No, I wasn't a special four-year-old kid, I was just extra-curious when I overheard the pastor talking about hell during a Sunday evening service. I can still feel the bumpy orange fabric of the pew under my coloring books as I doodled, my back to the stage. I can feel the sting on my kneecaps from my indented skin as it regained its form. I pulled myself off of the floor and into a big-girl seat on the pew when the pastor said, "hell", and "fire", and "forever." *Why would he talk about something that sounded so scary? Big people service was not nearly as fun as the kid's service and now they are talking about a dark place of fire and no God. Where is the candy? I need the green crayon.* I went back to my knees and that bumpy orange pew.

Lying in bed that night, I asked my dad what hell was and why the pastor was talking about it. I hadn't heard about it in my preschool class yet. He laughed because I was the curious kid with serious FOMO from the day I was born. He explained to me the reality, that even at four years old, I knew was the most important thing that I could know: God sent Jesus to rescue me from myself, from my sin.

"I really don't want to go there," I told him. Hell sounded awful, and heaven was the obvious choice. He explained to me with patient and loving words what it meant to let Jesus rescue me by receiving the rescue. He told me that

God didn't have to rescue me, but He did because He loves me so much. He gently told me that there was nothing I could do to get to heaven on my own without receiving salvation through my personal belief in Jesus. These were big concepts for a little mind, but it was in that conversation I realized that Jesus and His love could be mine to keep.

As I grew up, the authority of God and Jesus over my life never wore off, but the awe I had of their love and transformative power came and went. Each time I messed up as a teenager, I felt like I had disappointed God, so I would pray, cry, and repent, promising to never mess up like that again. It was a wash, rinse, repeat cycle. While the world would encourage me to brush off my mistakes, the Holy Spirit was close. He was drawing me back to Himself when I didn't have the strength. His work then was a part of the overall plan for my life.

By God's grace, my moments years later with Him in Odessa would unlock a joy in Christ I hadn't yet experienced. The Holy Spirit was preparing me to begin bearing fruit for the kingdom out of a famine season. All because I now understood that God was not just my Savior, but the Lord, Caretaker, and Sustainer of my life. As a result, I began hearing from God more regularly through His word. I also began knowing His prompts and discovering my purpose in obeying them. God is not a God of magic, hoping that people will figure out the trick. He is a God of invitation and when the Hero of life extends His love, the best choice that we can make is to receive it.

What About You?

How would your perspective change if you knew that your pursuit of self, more than a pursuit of God, actually stands in opposition to God and His plan for your life?

What would change about your relationship with God if you saw Him as your Lord (commander) and not just as your Savior? This book would prove to be a waste of time if we didn't take a moment to evaluate how we see God right now. In the desert, I had to choose to see God apart from my circumstances in order to see Him as Lord over my circumstances. I learned that I had to yield my life to God as the Hero of my story.

What about your lifestyle needs to change to reflect your dependence on your story's Hero? What social media accounts do you need to unfollow? What current self-care habits have you become dependent on? In what relationships are you spreading the fairytale beliefs rather than quenching them?

The real Hero is Jesus. And, because this is true, we get to walk with Him on a new path, one that looks quite different from the self-discovery journey of the fairytale. Tighten your ponytail, friends. We are heading out for our greatest adventure.

9 THE RESCUE

An Invitation to Rewrite the Script

In professional screenwriting terms, a rewrite is when you reopen a finished screenplay or pilot file and go back inside to alter or punch up parts of the dialogue, scenes, or the entire thing.

Some of our favorite movies were rewritten from their original script, leaving us to wonder how different our lives would have been had these final scripts never been changed. For example, according to the entertainment news source, Screen Rant, Monsters Inc. was originally written to follow the story of a 30-year old man who brings his childhood drawings of monsters to life to help him navigate his life experiences and emotions. The movie E.T. originally revolved around a band of en evil aliens who came to earth to destroy cattle while only one of them was good (Buddy). The Truman Show was originally written as a dark sci-fi thriller. Star Wars was originally written with a female hero, Han was supposed to be a green-skinned alien with gills, and Darth Vader was a bounty hunter.

Rewrites happen when the original script is important enough to write but isn't good enough to keep. Change is necessary when the original story doesn't land perfectly, when the characters don't fit, or when the ending doesn't fully resolve or satisfy the storyline. A rewrite is necessary to the movie when the screenwriter knows that the story will miss the mark.

Culture has written the script of a movie called "The Fairytale," pitching it to every woman, selling the story and the promise of a thrill of an impact if she will simply buy into its message. But Jesus says, "I've got the script that will blow the fairytale out of the water."

Jesus invites us into the "rewrite," into starting over, into a new beginning. A "rewrite" is offered to every person who has curiously dabbled in the water of self-love, getting dangerously close to the rip current. A "rewrite" is also for those who have been swimming out in the open waters of self as god for years.

The fairytale must be rewritten. There is no chance of our story resolving as complete or redeemed within the dead-end fairytale. But our rewrite isn't a project; it's an invitation. God as the screenwriter is offering to partner with you to show you the movie of your life as it should be written: with purpose, identity, and significance. His story for you far exceeds any box office and is one that, by God's grace, people will be talking about even into eternity.

The Message that Delivers: Salvation from Self

When we choose Jesus, we choose to follow the truth that delivers freedom. When we are caught up in the fairytale, we believe the message that "self" delivers us to a deeper and more important level of self. But the real message is this: salvation in Christ delivers us from self, not salvation to self.

Jesus is our Hero, wanting to do unforgettable things with our lives for His glory. This life is a journey of growing, seeking Him, failing, learning to repent and ask for forgiveness, and watching Him do things that only He can do in and through us.

As we understand the dangers of the fairytale messaging in culture and how we, like Alissa and Candace, can be swept away in its beauty, we also see that there is a flip side to the self-discovery journey. If there is a road that leads us to self as god and ultimately to spiritual death, then there is also a road that leads to spiritual life and fellowship with God forever.

This map wasn't created by a man or woman. It wasn't created by the universe or astrology. It's not innately woven into our being to somehow "unwrap" as we try to get to know ourselves. This map is of a journey with Christ, not a journey to self. A journey with Christ pulls us away from the mirror to see the glory all around us. Knowing Jesus means knowing the Destination. Knowing the Destination means walking confidently in the power of Jesus this side of heaven.

We have to starve the fairytale to see the new path for the journey. And, by God's grace, He partners with us in every rewritten stage of the journey. We are getting to the good part. I've already prayed this over you, so let's go. Let's look now at how Jesus wants to "rewrite the script" of the journey of self.

~~Self-Care~~
Loving Others and Loving God First

Too great a focus and effort on self-care becomes a lonely place to be. Our hearts were created to be with God and to be used for God. This life is not an individual sport. It's a team sport that requires us to love God and love others.

If you've been walking with Jesus for a long time, you may know this familiar feeling: you've studied God's word, joined the Bible study groups, you've listened to all of the Christian podcasts, and yet you still feel like there is something else you should be doing. There remains a missing piece. I've been here often, and the reality is that I get "fluffy" on information without using the information to impact the world around me. Just like we can consume too much food, without proper exercise, we feel the impact of the surplus of God's word in our life. We aren't purposed to consume without taking action. We start with Jesus, understand what He needs from us and for us, then we lace up our boots and get to work.

Yes, Christians, we can get so caught up in a form of Bible-focused self-care that we neglect to actually love others and God well by serving them with our lives. Self-care is the first step of the self-discovery journey, so as we flip the direction to see the healthy first step in living a life of freedom in our salvation, we have to turn our attention to God and to others. There is no other option. We maintain a healthy perspective of serving God and others when we understand that God's design for our life is that He gets the glory, and when we give Him the glory of our life, we experience our purpose in full.

We will feel fulfilled when God gets the glory. It's that simple. So will we step up in our God-given gifts and strengths to exercise what we know to be true about Him? Let's sit with 1 Peter 4:10-11 for a moment, then let's get to the work together; *"Each one should use whatever gift he has received to serve others, faithfully administering God's grace in its various forms. If anyone speaks, he should do it as one speaking the very words of God. If anyone serves, he should do it with the strength God provides, so that in all things God may be praised through Jesus Christ. To him be the glory and the power forever and ever. Amen."*

~~Self-Discovery~~
Knowing God

Saying yes to a journey of self-discovery without God means saying "no" to knowing yourself. Knowing yourself can only happen when you know your Creator. When you know Who designed you and that His love surpasses even your own ability and capacity to love, then you can see yourself in full. Like a completed puzzle, no pieces missing, no searching under the table to get a glimpse of what the unfinished work could be.

Knowing ourselves takes a lifetime while knowing God is an instant relationship and a lifetime of loving Him and learning about Him. You can see the heart of God and His plan and purposes when you open His word. Look at Ephesians 2:4-5, *"But God, being rich in mercy, because of the great love with which he loved us, even when we were dead in our trespasses, made us alive together with Christ—by grace, you have been saved."*

Knowing the God of miracles, Who resurrects lifeless and hopeless beings like me, humbles me to realize that this life is a privilege, and serving God is the highest honor.

~~Self-love~~
Sacrificial Love

Love is purposed to change us, not to exalt us. Love is supposed to be given, not only consumed. So many relationships fail because individuals are stuck in the mindset of "what can your love do for me?". The world has made love a gift only to receive, one that you can demand, distort, or dismiss however you wish. The world does not speak about love as a gift to be given because the enemy knows that if we get "fluffy" on self-love, we will forget about the real purpose of love: to give it away.

Sacrificial love is rare, but Jesus, Who was Love in human form, showed us what this looks like: "*By this we know love, that He laid down His life for us, and we ought to lay down our lives for the brothers*" (1 John 3:16). Sacrificial love may sound like a lot of work, and it may seem extreme for most people, but sacrificial love is the healthiest and most satisfactory kind of love because it's directly tied to the purpose of our existence. Sacrificial love changes the world. A life focused on loving self for the sake of loving self pulls us away from our real purpose and actually leaves us exhausted, tired, and never satisfied.

We move from self-love to sacrificial love when our hearts are changed by God. This part of our journey with God will change every part of us for the better. Sacrificial love can begin changing us today if we will live out of a heart like Jesus. Let's follow His lead on love as He's left us the instructions in 1 Corinthians 13:4-7: "*Love is patient and kind; love does not envy or boast; it is not arrogant or rude. It does not insist on its own way; it is not irritable or resentful; it does not rejoice at wrongdoing, but rejoices with the truth. Love bears all things, believes all things, hopes all things, endures all things.*"

~~Self-acceptance~~
Good Because God Makes Us Good

I'm in the fight of my life raising two daughters. It's not only critical for me to understand God's design of my worth and identity, it's critical for me to set my girls up for success to see it God's way, too. There are several great resources for young girls and teenagers to help them understand their acceptance and value in Christ such as Defined by Priscilla Shirer and *You're Worth It* by Shiela Walsh. But if I'm not leading by example, then the information can live in books, but not in their reality.

The enemy will use the same illusion on my two young daughters that he did on me, that he does for all of us. The illusion is that you can accept yourself fully and find wholeness in doing so. But there in the fine print that no one talks about is the reality that when you accept yourself fully, you have to accept the bad and the ugly about yourself. From there, you are then responsible for changing it all. However, you can't change everything about yourself. If you've fought for self-acceptance then you have to accept who you are and love the things you can't change. That doesn't sound terrible until you realize that the bad and the ugly parts that you can't change will keep you from ever being as good or better than the next woman. Exhausting. The comparison game takes you out quickly as you realize that self-acceptance only covers the societally acceptable "good" parts of us instead of turning to a God Who can remind you of your worth and Who can make you good.

The cross was proof that human beings cannot make themselves good. If we could, we would be living in a beautiful state of self-acceptance that didn't require trying to overlook the bad and ugly things that are like permanent markers scribbled on our lives. But Jesus left the perfection of Heaven to live 33 years on a broken, planet with sin-filled humans in order to make a way for us to be made new. He was the only One who could do it, so He is the only way to truly understand acceptance. The pursuit of self-acceptance ends at the cross as Jesus places His worth on us. 2 Cor 5:21 shows us the beautiful exchange, "*For our sake, He [God] made Him [Jesus] to be sin who knew no sin so that in Him [Jesus] we might become the righteousness of God.*"

With God, you don't have to find a way to accept the old you. God, out of His enormous love and mercy, makes us new the moment that we trust Him. 2 Corinthians 5:17 says, "*Therefore if anyone is in Christ, he is a new creation. The old has passed away; behold, the new has come.*" God invites us to lay down all of the bad and ugly parts of ourselves because making things new is His specialty. We don't have to accept what is sinful and broken in us; we can rather accept His acceptance of us and the new life He offers.

And now we walk boldly as new creations, understanding that nothing can change or impact our status of "worthy" because we were bought with a price and are eternally His.

~~Self-reliance~~
God Will [Really] Meet Every Need

Self-reliance seems like a good idea until it is held up to the light of the cross. If God made a way to meet our greatest need for righteousness and salvation from our sins, then He is most certainly also in control of the day-to-day needs of our lives. This life is beautiful, yet exhausting. We have a million things we need to think about and consider on a daily basis. Mental health is the most popular topic of choice right now because everyone is experiencing a decline on some level.

The pressure we know on a daily basis is sidelining us, too. The world says that we are strong enough to handle it; we just have to trust ourselves and believe in our own power. The greatest gymnast on planet earth, Simone Biles, did have power and was strong enough until she wasn't. At the 2020 Olympics, we watched her walk off of the floor to end her competition because of a mental block, putting her body in danger. Human limitations exist, and all the while God invites us into His unlimited storehouse of resources, power, and strength that He gives to us freely.

He doesn't look at us as sad, helpless human beings. He looks at us with compassion and love, a Father desperate to provide for His children, above and beyond what they need or deserve. The God-human relationship that He designed is one where God gives exceedingly and abundantly. Our role in the relationship is to give His gifts back to Him for His glory. Ephesians 3:20 isn't just an encouragement, it's a promise: *"God is able to do exceedingly abundantly above all we ask or think."* This is holy provision. God's providence is like cold water to an exhausted soul.

Sometimes, God's providence is simply His presence in a dark season of life, like my two years in the desert. God provided Himself for me when I was asking for a million other things. He Himself revived my spirit and gave me the strength to keep going.

So we set aside the striving and self-reliance filled with empty promises of culture, and we ask God for all that we need. We trust that His provisions are perfect in quality, quantity, and timeliness. His heart beats to the rhythm of faithfulness and generosity. We can trust His heart and His hands, and we can rest here too. Making the move from self-reliance to relying on God sets us free from exhaustion and striving. So we hand over the power and control we've held close and place it at His feet. With our lives feeling a million times lighter, we dance a new dance for our God Who provides.

~~Self as god~~
God as God

There can only be one God. No matter how flawless an influencer's Instagram account can look as it showcases a life that is self-started, self-made, and self-sustained, she is a human being who has to choose whether she will follow God or make herself the god of her own life.

We are fooled every day as we scroll our social media feeds. We are tricked into thinking that there are people who can have it all without having God. What we see outweighs the most important work: the work of the heart. What we don't realize is that God wants to do so much more for you than to give you the treasures of this world. The work of the heart is the transformation from God, leaving your old self behind and taking on our new title: child of God. But we will miss this if we are too concerned with establishing our own throne by means of success and significance. What is the condition of our soul? Do we want to be transformed by God or strung along by the world?

Success can't change our soul. Beauty can't change our soul. Confidence can't change our soul. Strength can't change our soul. Yet, we pursue these things with great intensity while neglecting deliverance, salvation, and redemption for the most important parts of us. On top of that, we claim that responsibility of salvation as our own. We believe that if we just do more, get better, love harder, or dig deeper that we will save our soul from despair. But there can only be one God. The creation is not more powerful than the Creator. The created are not more aware or conscious than the Creator.

We, the created, bow to the Creator and are indebted to Him for our very existence. We can spend our entire lives convincing ourselves that we deserve that spot on the throne of our lives, or we can give that seat to its rightful Owner. The message that sets a soul free is this: Acts 4:12 "'*Neither is there salvation in any other: for there is no other Name under heaven given among men, whereby we must be saved.*'" Newness exists in the life of Jesus Christ alone, not in a journey of self-discovery. Not in self-love or a consistent schedule of self-care. Our soul is hungry for God and His Presence. When the world says, "Do the work and trust your own power," God says, "I've done the work. Now come rest in all that I've created and planned for you to be."

10 THE COST

"Are you sure that you want to be done?" my mom asked me as we sat in the movie theatre parking lot. I was nineteen, and the conversation kept coming up as my mom and dad saw the struggle I faced and the stress that ravaged my body. Would I quit modeling and throw it all away? Or figure out a way to keep punishing my body into submission. I picked nervously at my fingernails and my eyes went back and forth, my head down in defeat as my brain searched for the right answer. I couldn't form tears from the exhaustion and numbness I felt toward it all.

I hated who I had become, and I had lost the girl that I once was. I knew that Jesus loved me, but what would other people think about me now? A girl too heavy to walk the runway. No one would know the model I had become because they could no longer see her.

The words felt like a white flag hitting the wind as they rolled out of my mouth, "I just can't do it anymore." My mind raced. Who would I be now? Was I crazy to walk away from this? What kind of life existed outside of this world? Would the admiration and applause stop? If so, where would I find it again? The cost felt impossibly high. But I also felt the indescribable peace of letting go.

The Cost Requires a Reality Check

The fairytale is filled with holes and cracks. The

more that our eyes are opened to the reality of the fairytale all around us, the more we understand that the enemy has taken the true, authentic, and righteous life through Christ and flipped it completely upside down, giving us a cheap and dead-end version of life. I pray, regardless of your current personal relationship with Christ, whether it's thriving or barely hanging on, that you're finding yourself aware of the fairytale all around you and ready to put up safeguards in your life to keep your focus on the bigger and better, which is always Jesus and the purpose He has given you to do big things for Him in this life. But, if you haven't already noticed, the world isn't very fond of anyone messing with their message of self-love, self-empowerment, and independence.

In fact, according to recent research, "The self-improvement industry statistics reported by Market Research state that by 2022 will have an estimated growth of $13.2 billion with 5.6% average yearly gains. Now, more than ever, people are focused on improving the quality of their lives by working on self-improvement."

This research also found that 70% of the self-improvement customers in the industry were women. In addition, research shows that 94% of Millennials are willing to spend up to $300 on their self-care every month.[14]

If I believe that Jesus is who He says that He is, and if I believe that my identity is found in the new creation that I was made to be at the moment of salvation, stamped with His love and forgiveness forever, then I cannot tell the world that it is quite right just as it is. The word "right" comes from the Old English root word "righteous" also meaning "morally correct." The world is not morally whole like God to start but broken by sin. Every person is born morally bankrupt. And, without God, each will die the same. People may believe that there is a "higher power" at play somehow but if the one true God is left out of the options, then anything we deem as "God" ends up circling back to us. The world will always

[14] Darko Jacimovic. "Top Self-Help Industry Statistics (Editor's Pick)." Deals on Health. Accessed June 22, 2021. https://dealsonhealth.net/self-improvement-industry-statistics/#:~:text=Commercial%20and%20medical%20programs%20 make,ones%20are%20worth%20%20%241.8%20billion

fight for itself because darkness hates the Light. But, as we've discussed, self without God stands in opposition to God.

The enemy has put on the makeup of self-love and a self-first society to cover up the blemishes, scars, wrinkles, and reality that every part of every woman, myself included—her mind, flesh, emotions, and will—has been corrupted by sin. Every woman stands in complete opposition to God until she receives His gift of salvation through Jesus.

By choosing Christ, our unseen Friend and Hero, there is a cost.

The Cost to Follow Jesus: Giving Over Control

Following Jesus means living weird and leaving a lot of room for people to question and be concerned about how hard you are swimming upstream. Following Jesus requires that we give up control over our lives. This sounds very cliche and "Christian." If you've been around long enough, "give God control" is a phrase used often. It connects deepest when we are walking through seasons where we have held onto control, therefore, giving it over to God is a spiritual and physical experience, unlike anything we've ever known.

I've watched women pray fervently over their unbelieving husbands for years, giving God full control over the outcome, only to see their husbands find Christ and follow Him faithfully. I've seen a woman, ravaged by Multiple Sclerosis, be the light within a room as she smiles, from her wheelchair, for another day that she can talk about Jesus and His love for her. I've heard from a young mom of three boys under three, who lost her husband suddenly, but gives God the glory for His life and gives Him control to help her raise her boys.

Control may be an over-used word, but it is the very thing that keeps us from experiencing the power of God. Jesus was fully submitted to the Father, giving Him full control. John 5:1 gives us a picture of their relationship, "*I am the true vine, and my Father is the vinedresser.*" Jesus' entire life and ministry were under the loving, merciful, and intimate control of God the

Father, just as it should be for us too.

Once we know the love of the Father, we know that He is the best Person to control our lives. From controlling our first breath to our last, His loving control over our lives changes every part of us. As we experience His transforming power in our lives, I pray that we will find ourselves praying daring prayers such as these:

"God, before you deliver me from this trial, deliver me from needing or depending on anything else that is not you."

"God, don't give me that peace I'm looking for until I find it in trusting You alone."

"God, don't bless anything in my life that is not surrendered to You."

These are prayers of women who get it. Until our lives are guided by our Creator, we will always live under the illusion of control, and we will see God as distant, not Deliverer.

The world is inviting us into deeper levels of control over our lives, while God is standing by, knowing what we need most and even giving us those things when we don't deserve them. He's not a country club God like many churches are today where you only get to benefit from the body if you're in that body. God still gives good gifts even when we avoid Him, dismiss Him, and take the credit for those gifts. Following Jesus means that we give up control as we realize how much better God's control is over our lives. It's a cost that is easy to give up when we know the Giver and Sustainer of life.

The Cost to Follow Jesus: Giving up Independence

The very last thing that you were designed to be is an independent woman. There is no greater privilege in this life than to depend on Jesus. To the world, giving up independence is foolish, but Jesus sees it as the only way for us to life and peace. So what does dependence on God get us? 2 Corinthians 1:21 tells us that as dependent Christians, God has anointed us (we've been empowered by God), that He has sealed us (we receive identity and protection), and that He has given us a guarantee through the Holy Spirit in us that is a promise of the future to come.

Independence sounds good until you realize that you have to do all of the work to find peace and significance in this life. Independence sounds good until you realize that you're working in opposition of the God who created you.

So here's what I know: you were designed to be stronger than yourself because of Jesus in you. You were designed to give more than you got because of Jesus in you. You were designed to live for more than you could plan because of Jesus and His mission written in your heart.

Giving up independence and living dependent on God will turn your struggle into rest and your striving into satisfaction. Your fragile heart will become whole in His name.

The Cost to Follow Jesus: Rethinking Influence

We're invited to a whole new way of life when we find Jesus. We are happy to give up the very things that we realize have kept us from His presence. We are happy to give up the things that tied us to ourselves to avoid living a self-elevated life. Giving up our biggest influencers means living opposite of that actual influencer that you see on your IG feed who constantly talks about self-love and affirmation without ever talking about what it means to serve other people. It means living the opposite of that influential pastor who preaches prosperity and big blessings for yourself when you do x, y, and z for the church. It means living the opposite of the hundreds of thousands of influential self-help books on the market. Our human examples of how to live our best lives have to change. Jesus needs to be our primary example of selflessness and humility. Philippians 2:3-4 says, "*Do nothing out of selfish ambition or vain conceit. Rather, in humility value others above yourselves, not looking to your own interests but each of you to the interests of the others.*"

Our lives were meant to be influential, yes, but if we are not influencing people toward God by reflecting His characteristics and priorities, then we are a part of the fairytale problem.

As Christ-followers, how we position ourselves in this conversation about the truth of the fairytale matters. How we respond to the marketing all around us, telling us how to put ourselves first, matters. How we live every day in our real, unfiltered, and important identity in Jesus everyday matters. We are influential, and people are watching.

There will be pushback. People won't know what you're doing or why you're choosing to believe and follow one God. People will be disappointed as you explain that pursuing a life of self is empty and that it misses the target of fulfillment and an intimate walk with their Creator. They don't want to hear that their efforts are like sugar water when God offers the remedy of living water to sustain our life. People will assume you're a piously religious person who is brainwashed by the Bible. Bottom line: people won't favor your stance on self-love and self-discovery, but people who heard Jesus in person 2,000 years ago didn't favor His stance on these things either.

I've held a quote by C.S. Lewis close as it has reminded me of the urgency of exposing the fairytale. Lewis said, "Jesus Christ did not say, 'Go into the world and tell the world that it is quite right.'" [15]

Imagine being able to influence someone toward eternal life with God instead of toward the season's hottest boots. Imagine influencing someone towards a fulfilling life with their Creator instead of a promising new diet program. You're meant to be influential. Be influential for God's eternal glory.

The Cost of Following Self

If you're looking to keep a peaceful, easy life that doesn't go against the grain or cause conflict, you only need to stick with the world on this one. The world has been sold a lie that following Jesus instead of ourselves costs us a life of fun and freedom. People don't commit to a church body because

---

[15] "C. S. Lewis Quote: 'Jesus Christ Did Not Say, "Go into the World and Tell the World That It Is Quite Right."'" n.d. Quotefancy.com. Accessed July 28, 2021. https://quotefancy.com/quote/780671/C-S-Lewis-Jesus-Christ-did-not-say-Go-into-the-world-and-tell-the-world-that-it-is-quite.

they can't tie themselves to a full belief system with all of its complexities, political stances, and its flawed people. The assumption is that if we follow a belief system that revolves around us, that feels good to us, and one that allows us to stay "true" to ourselves, that we will live a life of meaningful autonomy. No matter how beautiful the picture of meaningful autonomy seems, there is a cost.

Following Self Will Cost You Your Independence

Wait, didn't I just talk about how following the world will give you independence? How could that be? Well, independence is an illusion. As you choose self over God, you're still giving yourself over to someone, Satan. 2 Corinthians 4:3-4 says, "*And even if our gospel is veiled, it is veiled to those who are perishing. In their case the god of this age [Satan] has blinded the minds of the unbelievers, to keep them from seeing the light of the gospel of the glory of Christ, who is the image of God.*"

What exists is light and darkness, good and evil, God and Satan. If God does not have our heart, evil does, as it's our natural bend. If we do not rise above the sinful nature that we were born with, then we will continue to live in it, fully controlled by the "god of this age", Satan, who reigns over sinful human nature. So, no, living for ourselves is not an independent option. Following self costs us our independence and gives the enemy a whole lot more room to work, to move, to draw us closer to himself and further away from the light of God and His transforming love.

Following Self Will Also Cost You Your Peace

The idea of the self-discovery journey is to end up at a destination of wholeness and deep, inner peace that was living here all along. But the illusion is not a new one as the enemy has promised peace through many, many things since the very beginning. Peace through the forbidden tree in the Garden of Eden, peace through marriages, peace through sexual exploration, peace through having kids, peace through the right politician, peace through religious practices, and more. The enemy knows that he doesn't have to tempt us with any extreme measure to take our peace. He just has to tempt us to follow ourselves.

When we live self-obsessed, we forfeit the peace of knowing our truest selves. What I mean is that we can't actually know our truest selves without knowing God. God shows us who we really are: sinful and in need of a Savior. Then, He meets that need fully and completely by leading us to repentance and redemption and transforming our heart to look like His Son, Jesus. Our peace is made complete when we see Jesus in our reflection.

Following Self Will Cost You a Limited Love

We discussed selfless love vs. selfish love earlier and we unpacked what real love is and where it comes from. The highest value that the world chases by any means necessary is love, and without God, the enemy has convinced us that love is love by any definition. But love not received by us from God is a limited one. It's like seeing the world in black and white when God is inviting you to see love in color.

Ironically, a limited love says, "anything goes," with zero restrictions. It doesn't understand that love was given boundaries to protect broken humanity from distorting that which was designed by a Perfect God. A limited love puts a limit on forgiveness. A limited love shows favoritism. A limited love discriminates even when it thinks it doesn't. When we live in the love of God, we understand and live by that old saying, "the ground is level at the foot of the cross." Self-love can't give that much love away. 1 John 4: 20-21 says, *"If anyone says, 'I love God, and hates his brother, he is a liar; for he who does not love his brother whom he has seen cannot love God whom he has not seen. And this commandment we have from him: whoever loves God must also love his brother."*

My husband, Colston, says often to our church family, "You can only be loved to the depths by which you are known." We know most things about ourselves and our earthly existence but God knows much, much more about our existence. He thought us up, put us together, planned out our lives, knows our future, and gave us a choice about our eternity. God knows us best, so God loves us best. There aren't ten self-discovery lifetimes that could even come close to His unlimited love.

Following Self Will Cost You Your Eternity If You Don't Die to Self Before You Die

There is no greater love than the One Who laid His life down for us. There is a cost to following self, and we must understand that it is a cost much greater than simply not experiencing God on earth. You can't ignore God in eternity. You're either with Him in heaven or living in a dark existence thinking about Him forever. Describing hell, 2 Thessalonians 1:8-9 says, "*[it exists] in flaming fire, inflicting vengeance on those who do not know God and on those who do not obey the gospel of our Lord Jesus. They will suffer the punishment of eternal destruction, away from the presence of the Lord and from the glory of his might.*"

Living without dependency on God messes with the real after-life. And a life on earth without God? That cost is big, too. Eternity is a continuation of life with God, not the start.

The reality of human separation from God moved Jesus to do a lot of things, including giving His own life on the cross in our place. But, in Matthew 9:35-38, we see that as Jesus went from town to town teaching the people about God, he had compassion on them. The Greek word for compassion here is "splagchnristheis" which is the strongest known word or pity, meaning that Jesus' compassion moved Him to the deepest depths of His being. Why? Because verse 37 says that He saw the people like "sheep without a shepherd." Sheep without a shepherd is a reference to humanity being apart from God. Sheep without a shepherd are moving targets. They are in constant danger without a protector and guide. Sheep may be able to take care of their own basic needs, but without the Shepherd, they will be lost and vulnerable. Jesus cared deeply about our separation from Him for eternity, and He did something about it.

Alissa and Eternity

Alissa doesn't think much about eternity, but when she does, it scares her, so she chooses to believe that it will be a dreamy spiritual experience. After all, if she could find good in this life, how could the next life be bad? She has done her best to be a good person to others and chooses love when others would choose hate. That should count for something in today's world, right? Alissa believes that love is good and that no real love could produce a condemning hell that she's heard about from Christians. She chooses her truth and sticks to it. Nature is so beautiful, people are so beautiful, and life's opportunities are beautiful, too, so she busies herself with those things.

The cost she is paying is in full effect. Alissa may not feel the weight of her choice to go her own way and to live as though she can make God-sized decisions for herself, but that doesn't change the reality of eternity. The exchange, like the fairytale message, is subtle. The path is wide which leads to destruction, meaning that the world will support Alissa as she continues to white-knuckle for power and control.

The narrow road leads to life. The narrow road costs us the power and control for a reason; the Shepherd is there on the narrow path. He leads us down tight, overgrown, and heavily wooded spaces, avoiding the dangers of the wide-open roads. We avoid the heat of the sun and the dry gravel that is aching for a drop of water. The Good Shepherd knows where the streams of water run. He guides us while staying close and shows us the secrets of the path He chose for us. He points to the safest places to rest and sits with us as we renew our strength. He is the best company. The Good Shepherd knows that His guidance is far better than our independence, so He leads and we live safely and securely in His presence. We won't need a thing. We won't have to journey long and hard to find our purpose. Our purpose is to follow the Good Shepherd on the narrow path of life.

The Good Shepherd died for us so that we don't have to follow ourselves into the wilderness, losing sight of eternity and fellowship with God. Life begins on the narrow road with God and dies on the wide road of self. The cost is ours to choose. If we choose Jesus in our self-obsessed world, we choose life.

We've weighed the costs together. But I want you to know that as you choose God, the rest of your life is also in His hands. What I mean is that living for Jesus is possible today. On the day I resigned from my modeling agency in the movie theatre parking lot, I gave up a prestigious career that the world would consider a dream come true. I walked away from a life of achievement and money. Compared to the life I have now with Christ, I wouldn't go back for anything. Without Christ, any job or dream is dull, lifeless, and still missing the mark of joy.

Counting the cost and finding Jesus worthy is possible for you. Throw away the notion that God is looking for perfection and walk in the freedom that He is all about your surrender and redemption. As our world makes God a less-than-desirable option, remember the costs and remember His love that saw you from across the ravine and laid everything down to have you.

11 THE HAPPILY EVER AFTER

Candace called me about six months ago. She had seen a post in my Instagram feed that caught her off guard. The text graphic said, "You can't fully fix what you didn't create." The post started with this sentence: "We can figure out just enough about ourselves to make us think that we are in control." I could hear Candace breathing heavily as the wind blew into her phone. She was on a walk outside during her shift break as a nurse, which she often did when she was processing through bouts of heavy anxiety. She told me that she had been wrestling with God. "Emily, working in the Emergency Room during the COVID pandemic has changed the way that I see so many things, including myself," she said wearily. "Your post put words to the way that I'm feeling. I'm unable to fix the world around me or the storm that seems to always be brewing inside of me. I feel like I can only fix the way I feel when I numb out somehow, and I can only escape it for short periods of time." Her words felt like a confession, like she was laying down a bag of rocks, one at a time. She continued, "My coworkers are struggling too. A few of them have put signs around our break room that say things like, 'manage your energy, not your time.' or 'self-love is self-liberation.'"

I stayed quiet and listened. I could tell that she wanted to tell me more. Candace said, "But about a week ago I opened my Bible and read Psalm 139. I think God met me there, Em. He opened my eyes to see that, like, I matter a lot to Him." Her voice got shaky as she fought back tears. The Creator was speaking life into her through His Word, revealing His deep and ongoing pursuit of her heart to lavish her with His love. She realized that, as her Creator, He knew her better than she knew herself. She had made it to this day in her life without feeling fully satisfied in and of herself, although she had tried so many things to fill the empty spaces. The connection was made and Candace was seeing the truth and reality as God has meant for all of us to see it: that God is above it all. He is holy and righteous, yet personal and close. He is everything we could possibly need when we continue to fall short of ourselves.

She was quiet for a moment, then asked me, "What do I do next?"

I responded in the best way that I knew how. "Let God be God. Only He can do it best. Let Him lead, and partner with Him as He cares for you and works through your life." Knowing about her anxiety, I encouraged her to physically get on her knees before God at some point each day. "Tell Him everything, Candace." I explained that, based on my own personal wrestling with crippling anxiety, anything I held onto would become ammo for the enemy to use against me. "Remember that God is at work to save you from yourself, so don't go back. He is inviting you to trust Him. And, based on my personal experiences, trusting Him is the key to knowing the peace He offers."

Likewise, Asia connected with me on Facebook Messenger not too long ago. I had asked women for their input on a Facebook post as part of my research for this book. The question was "What is your perspective when you hear the term 'self-love'?". I had many responses come through and was thankful that Asia spoke up too. I knew about her love for Jesus and the Bible study that she leads. She had told me previously about the struggle she is facing in her group as women are leaning into the self-love and self-discovery practices and beliefs. These women wanted to know Jesus more but also felt pressure from the world to prove themselves as independent, strong, and self-sufficient college students, moms, and friends. Asia explained to them that the enemy is wildly smart. If he can't pull them away from God with darkness, he would use the light of familiarity and a love and devotion to themselves to distract them from Him.

Familiarity for women who know Jesus looks like this: messaging from the world that uses terms like "light," "life," and "love" outside of the context of God. Nothing is more confusing than a message that sounds like it's right, but isn't. Asia worries about these women and prays that God will give them discernment between the rip current of self-help and self-love beliefs and the truth of God's word. In her FB message to me, she explained her desperation to see women realize the fullness of who they already are in Christ.

"Christ has to be enough," she said. "We either decide that He is, or we continue pursuing ourselves to find answers that just don't exist in us." I was excited by her conclusion because the reality is that Christ is enough. He doesn't owe us signs or wonders to prove it. The real question is will we accept our true identity as His daughters? Or will we try to make something else of ourselves?

God doesn't have competition because no one can reach His level. We can live our lives as god wanna-be's, or we can live for Him as the women we really are when we choose Him: heiresses. As Romans 8:17 says, "*Now if we are children, then we are heirs—heirs of God and co-heirs with Christ, if indeed we share in his sufferings in order that we may also share in his glory.*"

Choosing to live opposite of the fairytale and of the world is radical. We won't teach our children to love themselves most but will instead show them what it looks like to love God and to love others to live the most fulfilling lives. We won't simply nod our head in agreement with a friend who is disregarding her faith and choosing to find her way through New Age practices and self-help talk. We won't bow down to a self-obsessed culture by deconstructing our faith to come to our own conclusions about God and the world we live in.

Changing God's narrative to the fairytale is the enemy's greatest scheme, and most people have fallen for it. The enemy has stolen away from people's ability to get in close proximity to

God because they've "puffed up" their own lives so much that there is now a canyon of space between them and God. By His grace, He fills canyons of space and caverns of hearts when one seeks Him with all her heart (Jeremiah 29:13).

Raising Girls

Whether we are raising daughters or helping friends and family raise theirs by our love and support, we've got work to do. The fairytale is already written for them, and the world has a custom "me" plan for them; if they are not confident, the fairytale of self tells them to be confident in every part of them, including their flaws. Meanwhile, God invites them to find confidence in Him. This allows them to take their eyes off of their flaws and onto bigger and better things such as understanding their purpose and significance in Him. Let's not give our girls one more thing to have to overcome. Let's not ask our girls to try to find the beauty in the broken every day when God offers to take their hand and show them who He has made them to be.

We raise our girls well when they understand that the world is meant to revolve around God and His glorious purpose for them. We raise our girls well when they don't spend their lives looking in a mirror but to the example of Jesus Who served and loved people. We raise our girls well when they know that their identity has nothing to do with what they look like, who they love, what they do, or where they go. Their identity is found in their "yes" to their Creator. It's a daily habit of showing them how to pursue God instead of self: growing in the knowledge of God in His word, giving time and energy to other people, and going wherever God leads.

Our girls need us to lead them now more than ever before. As social media, friends, and culture feed them the fairytale, we must fuel them with the truth. They are not as the world paints them to be, and they are not loved by the world. They are loved and treasured by God who knit them together and gave them a chance to live a big, beautiful and meaningful life.

Leading Friends and Family

Here's where the deepest ache of the fairytale can exist for us: watching our friends and family interact with the journey of self while knowing that the truth of God's love and sovereignty is what will actually set them free. We don't want to rock the boat, but if the boat is on the waters of the fairytale, it's already sinking.

How do you speak to a lifetime of selfish living? How do you reveal the truth of the fairytale to those who seem to love living in it? How do you expose the scheme of the enemy when the scheme is most culturally relevant?

Remember that the god of this age, Satan, is working hard to keep people blind: "*The god of this age has blinded the minds of unbelievers so that they cannot see the light of the gospel that displays the glory of Christ, who is the image of God*" (2 Corinthians 4:4). We get the privilege to pray for these people in our lives, that God would open their eyes and soften their hearts toward Him. One passage in Acts showcases God's ability to do this: "*One of those listening was a woman from the city of Thyatira named Lydia, a dealer in purple cloth. She was a worshiper of God. The Lord opened her heart to respond to Paul's message*" (Acts 16:14). With prayer and boldness, we present the truth: "*How, then, can they call on the one they have not believed in? And how can they believe in the one of whom they have not heard? And how can they hear without someone preaching to them?*" (Romans 10:14).

They may see deeper revelations of self as the pathway to freedom, but the idol of self is slavery to sin. Romans 6:6 tells us, "*We know that our old self was crucified with him in order that the body of sin might be brought to nothing so that we would no longer be enslaved to sin.*" Conversion to the life God offers requires ending a life of slavery to sin through confession to the Father, faith in Jesus Christ, and becoming a slave to righteousness, offering one's body as a living sacrifice.

Talk about and expose the messages of culture that exist all around us. Show them the self-focused marketing that is driving people inward. But don't just point out the flaws of the world without giving them the Solution. Get brave and be bold. Talk about Jesus as you know Him; how has He flipped the script for you? How has Jesus saved you from yourself so that you can live on mission and with significance that impacts eternity? Invite your girlfriends to start having this conversation. Start a small group, meet for coffee, be willing to vulnerably open up about your own experience with the fairytale. We will change when we begin starving the fairytale together.

More than anything, I want the women in my life to know who they are in Christ and who they can be when they choose Him. I want them to know that they were meant to live in closest proximity to the Father, not themselves. I want them to know that He will change their lives in every way. So I'm working on being that friend for them, the one who cares enough to say something, to say the right thing, to speak the truth of God over them.

Leading at Church

The Body of Christ needs to tackle the fairytale head-on. Too many people in our body are living with a little bit of Jesus and a whole lot of self. How do we help them see that Jesus alone really is enough?

We meet them right where they're at. What I mean is that each person who follows the fairytale is drawn to it for a reason. If they are a perfectionist, like Candace, they are likely drawn to the fairytale because it promises acceptance when you accept yourself just as you are, flaws and all. If they hate the way that they look on the outside like I did, the fairytale will promise freedom through the choice to love themselves at all costs. If that person is riddled with trauma, then the fairytale promises freedom when she begins peeling back the layers of her life and speaks self-affirming words over each layer. If that person deals with any aspect of mental health, the fairytale promises freedom if she'll simply speak her own truth and follow whatever feels best to her regardless of the world around her.

Leading at church means approaching people just like

Jesus did, on a case-by-case basis. The fairytale draws people in based on their life experiences and promises a remedy for a specific hang-up. Our job is to lean into their lives, understand where the brokenness lies, and show them the antidote found in the love and mercy of their Creator.

Happily Ever After

I believe that the closing credits of our lives will mean a whole lot more than we think they will. Our story will end with a life that either pursued self, or God in the daily grind. The name that is written after "directed by" and "written by" determines a lot more than just where we will spend eternity. That name determines the quality and significance of your life right now as you're holding this book in your hands. You and I will answer to God for this moment in time, and every other moment that we've existed. Every breath counts.

So in the final breaths of this book, if you have counted the cost for what it means to follow Christ and partner with Him as He rewrites the script of the journey of the self, I want to encourage you. This is the "happily ever after" available to you:

You can (really, truly, and fully) rest in your God-given identity. Breathe it in!

You are God's most prized possession.

You are already enough because Jesus paid the penalty that you couldn't.

Your life is meant to deliver a daily dose of God and His love for the people all around you; this purpose alone will satisfy the longing of your soul.

Your experiences are meant to draw you closer to the Father like the intimacy of a tried and true friendship.

You will shine brightest when you reflect the immeasurable grace of Jesus.

Every detail of your life, of your feelings, and of your emotions matters to God, and He knows exactly what to do with them. To know Jesus is to know Peace and to actually live each moment with that peace.

With Jesus, you can stop searching, working, and striving. He is the Answer.

Starving the fairytale every time you encounter it, fueling your life with truth, and living in and for the glory of God's goodness will make for a life best spent. He is the Hero, and He is everything you've been journeying to find and so much more.

ABOUT
EMILY COPELAND

Emily is a pastor's wife and mom of two girls (and one giant dog) from southeastern Michigan. She is a copywriter by day and is always on the hunt for the next best iced americano. Even more so, she is an enthusiastic encourager of women, praying that they will place their hearts and lives into Jesus' hands. *Starving the Fairytale* is Emily's first book.

Made in the USA
Columbia, SC
03 July 2022